Cardiff Libraries
www.cardiff.gov.uk/libraries

Llyfrgelloedd Caerdyd
www.caerdydd.gov.uk/llyfrgelloe

D1076319

THE AFFAIRS
OF OTHERS

Amy Grace Loyd is an executive editor at *Byliner Inc.*, and was the fiction and literary editor of *Playboy* for over six years until 2012. She has also worked in *The New Yorker*'s fiction department and was associate editor on the *New York Review of Books* Classics series. She has been a MacDowell and Yaddo fellow. She lives in Brooklyn, New York.

THE AFFAIRS OF OTHERS

Amy Grace Loyd

Weidenfeld & Nicolson
LONDON

First published in Great Britain in 2014
by Weidenfeld & Nicolson
An imprint of the Orion Publishing Group
Orion House, 5 Upper St Martin's Lane, London WC2H 9EA

An Hachette UK Company

1 3 5 7 9 8 6 5 4 2

© Amy Grace Loyd 2013

All rights reserved. No part of this publication may be
reproduced, stored in a retrieval system, or transmitted,
in any form or by any means, electronic, mechanical,
photocopying, recording or otherwise, without the prior
permission of both the copyright owner and the above publisher.

The right of Amy Grace Loyd to be identified as the author of
this work has been asserted in accordance with the
Copyright, Designs and Patents Act 1988.

All the characters in this book are fictitious, and any resemblance to
actual persons living or dead is purely coincidental.

A CIP catalogue record for this book is available
from the British Library

978 0 297 87118 7 (cased)
978 0 297 87119 4 (trade paperback)

The Orion Publishing Group's policy is to use papers that are natural,
renewable and recyclable products and made from wood grown in
sustainable forests. The logging and manufacturing processes are expected
to conform to the environmental regulations of the country of origin.

www.orionbooks.co.uk

To Jerry and Suzanne,
my first great loves

I've known you for years. Everyone says you were beautiful when you were young, but I want to tell you I think you're more beautiful now than then. Rather than your face as a young woman, I prefer your face as it is now. Ravaged.

—Marguerite Duras, *The Lover*

Some people set themselves tasks
other people say do anything only live
still others say
    oh oh I will never forget you event of my first life
                          —Grace Paley, "Life"

HOPE

————

THE BODY OF A WOMAN aging. It's a landscape that, even as it vanishes, asks a lot of the eyes. Or it should. No two landscapes the same. They never were the same, no matter their age, but then how time brings details to the body.

Of course every woman's body ages. What's disorienting is how friendly it all starts out, with words like smooth and tight and firm, high and pink and wet—words that are given to women's bodies and that they wear around, as comfortably as cotton. And why not? These are gifts they did little to earn. Life does this so rarely—offer unearned or unasked-for rewards. But inevitably the words fall away, one by one: There goes tight, there goes smooth, god, even wet. And the words that replace them, that are provisioned, are not nearly so welcome or easy to carry. Some women carry these new ways of addressing their bodies with pride. They'll explain that the knots in their flesh tell a good story. Others celebrate the change of vernacular, the end of a certain kind of surveillance. Or they continue to pursue the first set of words—high, tight, smooth. It's not wrong or it's not for me to say. Who am I to say? I am a young or youngish woman. I am in my late middle thirties, though I could be twenty-five or fifty. I believe I have no age anymore. I am not unattractive but neither am I beautiful. I married a man I first met in college and then again later, a few years after graduation. My husband died a difficult death. I went with him, or a lot of me did. I cannot apologize for this nor do I wish to challenge that I am changed.

Being a widow was a respected thing once. Understood as a destination. Now, we are asked to let go, move on, become someone or something else, marry, divorce, marry again. American life asks us to engage in an act of triumphant recovery at all times or get out of the way. I have been happy to get out of the way.

My husband left me comfortably provided. With the money given me, I bought a small apartment building in which I live and rent three one-bedroom apartments. Behind my building in downtown Brooklyn there is a garden of three hundred square feet with an old lilac bush that blooms a deep ancient-looking purple, a tall female ginkgo, a scrawny sycamore, and then a strange assortment of plantings to which the previous owners and I have made a halfhearted commitment. In my case I queried will this herb or flower grow, and if the answer was yes, I let it make its bid for survival and maybe even return on its own the following year. I am often surprised by what greets me in the spring. Weeds of course but also a determined patchwork of grass that reminds me of the head of a disheveled balding man. My tenants have asked to contribute to the garden, but as I am not here to make a family of them, to know them too well, I've not encouraged this and so their relationship to the garden is as tentative as it is to me. I have only been a landlord for four years.

I didn't normally allow subletters, but George brought her, a candidate, to meet me on a day where, though it was only the beginning of March, I could smell the soil in the damp air and had noticed the daylight was lengthening. George had always been a good tenant. He lived above me on the second floor and was careful of the noise his feet made over my head, and once when I was ill with a bacterial bronchitis, he had gone to pick up my antibiotics at the drugstore for me. He taught English at St. Ann's, a private school on Pierrepont Street that turns its students into sophisticates long before they can vote, and he had published poems in journals meant to impress the literate. He was gay and had had a roommate initially, a lover of many years who left him after only a few months of living in my building. At night, during that time, when I couldn't sleep, I heard George walking the floorboards, the same length, back and forth and back and forth, as if he were schooling himself in precision. If I focused on his regular steps, the predictable shifts his weight made, I would fall back to sleep, his vigil excusing me from my own. Once I heard him cry out—it sounded like someone had startled him. I immediately thought of a ghost, perhaps of himself, when he loved and was loved.

I had seen the woman to whom George wanted to let his place on the streets of Brooklyn Heights and Cobble Hill alone or sometimes in the company of people I took to be her family. She had broad shoulders for a woman and long legs, though she was not overly tall, only a little above average in height. I could have mistaken her for French— her clothing, her unapologetic femininity, the dark lipstick and the way she swept her hair up on her head and into a twist—but the accent, the volume and pace of her voice, and the openness of her face didn't fit. It would be fair to say she was beautiful. Last fall, I was sure I had seen her with a young man on Hicks Street, on a deserted residential block. I had felt I was intruding and crossed to the other side of the street. I took him to be her son because he resembled her—same color hair, same body type. She grabbed him abruptly and hugged him with all of her, as if she were trying to steady him against a mean wind or force something out of him. That day, I remember I thought *sorrow,* she's trying to hug his sorrow away and there was no time to lose apparently. When she let him go, she looped her arm in his, and they walked away vividly in step, in league, heads high, not embarrassed or worried about who might have seen them, but full of vitality and purpose. I believe I am remembering that right or that is how I want to remember it.

She had left an impression or several, and it was a pleasant enough association.

George wanted to go to France for a time to see an ailing friend. He wanted to get away, to write. He talked very briefly about the sensuality of time and of landscape, the sort that can't be had in America, in New York City, and then he talked about Marseille, the city, and Rimbaud—did I know Rimbaud? He talked more quickly than he might usually, which was all to say he wanted out, urgently, but eventually he wanted to come home to Brooklyn, to his apartment. He'd arranged a leave for the rest of the school year and then he had the summer off anyway— the great boon of teaching, he said, summers. There was simply the matter of the apartment, of rent, of me. He could not afford to go if I did not let his dear friend Hope stay for a while. He didn't slow down or acknowledge how a body might respond to the words "let Hope stay." He kept talking, launching his hope at me with her there beside him nodding brightly at intervals, and it was my duty to demonstrate some resistance. I had some but not much. My tenants think me cold. They know that I am young or youngish, but some part of them does not believe it.

I began by explaining how small the building is, how

careful I am in selecting my tenants, that there is a certain consonance of character I look for and mean to maintain.

George offered, "Of course, I would not suggest anyone who I didn't think suitable."

Then I brought up precedent, my desire for consistency; at this Hope craned toward me and spoke to me as if English were my second language.

"But I am a friend of George's and the neighborhood's, was it Ms. Cassill?"

Her lipstick looked expensive and her brows were dark and high in their natural arch. She knew the impact her face could have, even now in her mid- to late forties. She'd known it for years.

"It's Mrs., and I don't doubt that you are—"

"I'm sure the other tenants could be made to see—"

"With that, it's tricky—"

"Is it really? Huh." She changed course, biting down on her lip to contain her enthusiasm. "Did George ever tell you that I'm a great cook?"

"Are you?"

"George would probably eat better in his own kitchen with me running it than in France."

"Well, that's something—"

"Why don't you let me cook for you?" She was trying to flirt with me.

"Very kind but not at all necessary."

She was the sort who created intimacies where there were none.

"I could cook a meal for the whole building if you'd like and serve it out there in that lovely garden. Pâté and bouillabaisse and good bread and wine, a great mess of a meal—"

"We don't really have . . ." I threw a look at George. Flattened my tone. "No, that's not at all—*necessary*. I wouldn't dream of asking that of you or my tenants. We are very respectful of each other's—what? *Separateness* here . . ."

Her face, which had been full of expectancy, fell slightly, and I saw her age there, a feathering over the upper lip; two sharp lines that had dug in and stayed between her brows, but on a face with good bones and wide planes and eyes so light, an almost yellow blue, these lines gave her a helpful gravity, an authority. She'd run out of the energy it takes to be playful quickly, more quickly than I'd have guessed. She shook her head at George and then opened her arms and shrugged. "Not a good year so far, darling."

He placed an arm on her shoulder. Placed it because he was gentle with her, wanted to show her gentleness. "It's been a hard go," he said.

Looking at me with some impatience now, and taking in a big breath, he was about to launch another appeal when Hope, straightening her neck and leveling her shoulders, making the best of her height, preempted him: "I'll pay for the whole thing up front, security included. Cash. Does *that* interest you?"

"Money's not really the issue here. Is it Miss or Mrs.?"

She smoothed her light brown hair on one side above her ear and looked down to inspect her sweater. It was sage-colored and looked handmade, with a silk-cotton thread. It flattered her. "I left my husband, you see. I need a safe place. A quiet place. I thought this was it. George and I thought . . . well"—she put her hand on George's forearm—"we're like children, I suppose. We thought it would all fall together. That something could." Tears bloomed through those strange eyes, and she laughed a little. "George and I both need new scenery, but there are other options, aren't there, George? We needn't trouble you anymore." With a stiff hand, she patted at my upper arm, letting go of me and the conversation utterly. I was no one to her. I had been an obstacle to overcome and that's all. "C'mon, George. Let's go find a drink."

"Celie, really," he said to me. He had never called me "Celie," only "Celia," my name in fact and what I prefer to be called. "I can't afford to cover the rent while I'm gone. And I have to go away. I really *have* to. Do you really want to go to the trouble of getting a new tenant, of evicting me?"

I took a moment. I pretended this was something I hadn't considered. I had always planned on saying yes, but he had to know, as she had to know, that this was my home first, theirs only by concession, and with some formality; a place here had to be earned. I was responsible for the roof, the boiler, the cast-iron plumbing. I had refinished all the floors, had sanded and painted the walls, and rehung all the doors. This building in all its particulars, even securing the building permits from an unhelpful urban bureaucracy for the renovation of the entrance and windows, readying the old cable elevator for inspection, had given me purpose when I was newly widowed. I'd claimed it with intentions I didn't even fully understand. Yes, a safe place. Order. For me and others on the other side of walls, of floors, tenants I would and would not know. A city arrangement on my terms for as long as I stayed in the city.

I had hired help of course, but I worked alongside Anton and his wife, Marina, and his brother, sometimes their son, Ukrainians all. They were hardworking and did not complain, at least to me, about my insisting to participate in the work. My muscles remembered every effort still, and I could see my contributions everywhere around me. My mistakes, too, though these weren't appreciable. I'd been careful, and I believed the building and I had an agreement. We would keep each other well.

I'd extend myself for my tenants but only so far.

I called to Hope, who had moved to the door, her long back to me. "Can you take care of plants? George has so many. You even have an orchid or two, don't you, George? They're temperamental."

George nodded.

"I've taken care of George's watering here and there when he's gone on shorter trips," I said.

"She has," he said. I could see the pleasure welling in

him. He was a neat medium-sized man with a broad face that always reminded me of actor James Mason's; it was soft and hard, gentlemanly but acute, and it colored easily. He was forming a paunch and had begun to belt his pants higher.

"I've not killed anything." Hope gave us her profile first. "Or anyone," then she turned and smiled with her whole body, "yet." She laughed low to high, arriving at something like a giggle, and then threw her arms around George. When she released him, she looked at me full in the eyes. She went to touch me but thought better of it this time, out of respect, I suppose, and steadied a look on me so grateful and unshy with relief that I barely heard her "thank you" or listened to the details of her arrival. I've only known one person who could focus on a body so completely, with such sincerity, and he was gone.

As they opened the door to go, she ran back to me and grabbed my hand. "Not to worry. I will try to behave myself." I smelled her then. She wore a perfume or deodorant that was floral and spicy. Rose and rosemary or smells like these, at odds and in sympathy, that bring to mind a versatile garden, and spring. It was light but present, and her hand covering mine was soft and hot. "You have made us so happy."

FERRY CAPTAIN

———

WITHIN A WEEK her scent filled my building—a week of scuffing and scratching, lugging and rearranging above my head. That was George preparing to go. He moved almost constantly and when he stopped for a bit, there would come a burst, a racing toward some object, I thought—a forgotten piece of clothing. Or maybe he startled himself with the thought of a book and whether it was worth bringing. Hope came and went during this time, carting in bits and pieces of her life, her arms circling a garbage bag of what could have been clothes or her own linens, a plant, a reading lamp, with more to come. I did not always see her during these visits, but I heard her voice, the sound of her feet, lighter but as ungovernable as George's had become overhead, and I smelled her or I swore I could. Yes, given my responsibility, I was sensitive to my environment, but surely my other tenants had noticed the activity; perhaps George had told them of the change.

The Braunsteins, my tenants in apartment three, were an excitable pair, a modern couple, teeming with plans. Not so Mr. Coughlan, my tenant on the fourth floor. He would not make much of Hope's arrival, or only briefly. He had been a merchant marine and then a ferry captain all over the Northeast. I usually saw him coming or going on his walks in the morning, when he was full of the new day, his life and its particulars popping in his head, in his body, already. Once he had saved a seven-year-old boy who'd fallen overboard from drowning; he'd kept an epileptic in full fit from swallowing her tongue. Another time a fallen tree branch caught in the boat's rudder had nearly put his ferry out of commission, but he had prevented that. With me and I'm guessing with others, Mr. Coughlan was often pleading his case; eighty-two is not too old when you know so much or more than most captains today. He did this without aggression. He had too much joy and expanse in his recollections, and he had a great capacity for quiet, for enjoying it, even parsing it. When he was particularly nostalgic and finally at home in my company, and me in his, he'd pause and try to give me some sense of the full fresh air he'd known, of the life growing in an engine, and even of the sounds he missed, without theatricality. "Out there," he'd say, "you have to be awake," yes, for the pounding and spraying, the shushing and sluicing—all that energy, motion, and promise around him daily; and the men, their names out of old movies, Gus, Bud, Ike, who were better on boats than anyplace else. Company lost to him now—or almost, because he still lived it, the sounds and voices, here, upstairs, in my building.

When he appeared at my door four years ago, I knew nothing about him and he didn't offer much. He wore gray wool trousers and a seersucker jacket that was lightly stained on the breast pocket. His clothes were pressed and his salt hair was combed and brilloed into place. He'd shaved too, but on a face so weathered it didn't do much in the way of brightening or smoothing. He had hazel eyes that squinted from the anticipation of glare. He was no more than five foot eight.

He made his pitch to me in a very considered way. He said he was staying at a place down the road he did not much care for. Family had provided it for him, which was kind, but it was not for him. "Too many people lining up just to park themselves in front of the TV. The food has no flavor, the windows are dirty, and everything is covered in plastic." He'd passed by my building on his walks and wondered if I had a room. I said I did, though I wasn't looking for tenants just yet. He nodded at that and offered me six months' rent, cash up front. "No one has to know," he said, smiling at me with his eyes, "but us." I couldn't make out any alcohol on him and he did not look away from my face once. His body looked sturdy for a man of his years, and his stance on shortish legs was wider than most people's as if he expected the ground to buck up beneath him. It didn't seem like he was one to complain if it did; he was simply ready. He breathed through his nose; it was audible but steady. When I hesitated, he stuck his big mottled hand at me. It was alive with blue veins. He let it hang there until I shook it.

He wanted the fourth-floor apartment. It was my smallest, with lower ceilings than the rest, but it wasn't from modesty that he picked it when I gave him the tour; it was for the view. Out of one western-facing window, to the back of the building, there was a slice of the New York Harbor on offer. Another gave him some uninterrupted sky. He went back and forth between those two windows a few times, gauging to make sure he got the sights right. It was then something told me he would die here, in this one-bedroom apartment, and that was what he was deciding, whether it would be okay. I wanted to take our agreement back then—a seam of panic folded my stomach in two—but I didn't. I took his money and lied to his daughter, the family to whom he'd referred, when she came round fuming and pointing fingers in my face. Her father and I had an agreement, I told her without hesitating, and I had no intention of going back on it. She'd had him in an assisted living facility. His various pension payments and social security were meant to go there, not to me. I had simply replied, "What a shame."

I could not explain that I understood better than she did where he really lived, in *Then*—when he was most alive. I also knew that he'd never trouble me, or not intentionally, and whatever my relationship with my other tenants, he and I would never quarrel over hot water or light fixtures.

I climbed the stairs to his apartment now. His door was never locked, though I had cautioned him about that. I knocked, but he had his radio going at a volume that was meant to keep him awake. I knocked again, then went in. He'd tucked himself into his wood-and-leather recliner beside a fragile end table that gave legs to the radio bellowing the tide report. He looked too stony in his sleep until the third or fourth breath, when a snuffing exhale rattled him and made his fingers twitch. He was dressed in worn black boots with rugged soles, work pants, and a wool sweater, a favorite outfit of his and the same one he wore in a photo I'd seen, taken years ago, in which he gave a low, two-finger salute from a ferry wheelhouse. The windows of his apartment were all opened. While it was mild for March, it was not warm. I shut all but one of the windows, and that I left open a crack. I checked to see if there was food in the fridge. I found unspoiled milk, some cheddar cheese, and white bread tied tight into formation. In his cabinet were four cans of soup, two of which I had dated with pen on another visit. I surveyed the kitchen and living room area (which were joined and separated by a granite-topped island I had installed) for signs. There was an unwashed bowl and spoon in the sink. The nautical charts he hung on the walls with tape were crooked, but they'd always been.

I smelled for something rotten or sick or dirty, but there was nothing, or nothing I could smell; then I left, shutting the door I'd oiled and re-oiled quietly behind me. He had reassured me again, by doing so little.

PARTY GREETINGS

ON SATURDAY, THE NIGHT BEFORE George was to leave, a party formed overhead. Music. Laughing. Protests. Exclamations. More laughing. I counted at least ten or so bodies by way of voices and feet. Edith Piaf cried out for them—strident, demanding—until she was replaced with the bland bass lines of what I took to be house or lounge music. Aromas of garlic and thyme and onions came to me; and I made out lamb and baked cheese, sharp and oily. I had a bottle of Veuve Clicquot for George. Chilled. I had been invited upstairs but had not yet decided to go. I heard my elevator in use—the mechanical effort begun with a shudder and then the hum that comes with its duty, a vibration in the walls. The tenants mostly used it when they had things to carry. Mr. Coughlan used it when he could admit that he was tired. I heard more doors opening and shutting. The entrance door and others. Agitation had its way of spreading. Footfalls tapping, the floors continually adjusting. Hellos hallooing. There's a certain pitch to party greetings. It aims high; it's grateful and hopeful. I had an ear for it from years of watching my mother throw parties. No matter how many times she'd been disappointed, she still believed a party could be transformative, could suspend time and place.

I knew I could not pass into the party upstairs unseen, but I could wait until just after the crescendo; a few departures, a slowing or cessation of moving feet, the adjusting of furniture. They might turn down the music at this stage, too, or switch it to a vocalist whose singing went well with port or cognac, but then maybe I was expecting too much of them.

When I judged that moment had arrived, I combed my hair. Dusted my face with some powder. I wore an Irish sweater and jeans. I had not worn a dress or forgone clothes designed for comfort in ages. I was going to be polite, not to impress, though I did search out a Chanel lipstick sent by my mother in a care package of assorted female encouragements. Red; it smelled of sweet clay and roses.

I am just passing through, I told myself, I am a voyager, a ghost, a spy—my mother teased me with this when I used to trail her around. *A spy.* She said it with exasperation and love. The lipstick: Yes, it conjured my mother, who debated every detail before her parties, the food, the glassware, the quality of the light in the rooms of the Victorian in which we lived. At the end of her preparations, she'd dress hastily in an outfit laid out earlier in the day.

I grew up in southern Connecticut, in a bedroom town so pale and post-collegiate you'd think Cheever made it out of whole cloth. The population's imagination was only big enough to try for variations on normalcy and levels of acceptable wealth. But my mother, who grew up in Northampton, a university town in Massachusetts, went in for clothes that were beaded, flared, or crocheted. She had vivid silks and authentic kimonos. She served canapés and fromage de chèvre. She liked museums and Manhattan at night and dancing till her feet bled. And she had short waves of honey blond hair, cleavage, and big violet eyes given to surprise, to teasing. I inherited none of these things. She was high even before the champagne was opened and then she was flying, not of the earth, certainly not of that town and its family cars and duck shoes, or determined not to be. My father didn't care for the parties much. That people became more interested in him as he rose in the world of New York finance necessitated that he become more reserved in social situations. He drank a few fingers of scotch and he watched my mother for signs that she'd had too much. When that moment arrived, and it did more often than not, he'd call me from my room or wherever I was holed up, and together we'd begin clearing the plates, offering coffee, washing what we could. We'd turn the music down; we didn't refill their glasses or their cups. We rushed the party along so that we might have her back, to ourselves. We were cordial, but we hated all those people at a certain point. We hated them for their greed, for the mess they left us, and for the state the night left my mother in. When the house was still again, she fell into belligerence, carping. In part we could thank the wine for that, but more she could not bear the quiet now that she'd been elsewhere.

George's door was left ajar. I pushed into an altered space. There was nothing but candles for light, long and short shadows thrown everywhere, dancing occasionally with a current of air caught in this flame or that. What you couldn't see in George's apartment now was how much he subscribed to neatness. Over the length of his stay with me, he had replaced objects of convenience, bought in grad school, with carefully chosen ones, some new, some antique, but all with alert lines and architecture to them. He'd had bookshelves built in to accommodate this collection. We'd split the cost. He was proud of his brown leather couch with its shapely mahogany legs; there was also a Mission floor lamp with a leaden glass shade—he'd called me up to see it the day after he brought it home. I assumed he wanted to point out a problem with the apartment, an electrical outlet, the toilet; that was more like it.

Instead, he asked me to look at his lamp and so I did, the micaed bronze of the stand, the strong geometry of the shade's design, its weight. He was quiet until he said it reminded him of the men he used to fall for—no loud frills, solid, but elegant. I remember he added "unmistakable," though at the time I was caught on "used to," as though he was aligning himself with the likes of me or Mr. Coughlan.

He preferred muted colors, and he left empty, navigable spaces between objects. Even his plants were not allowed to fraternize with one another; each had its place, its part in the layout.

I had come to think in his case that the impulse toward spareness was an invitation, an optimism, leaving room for others or, on days when life felt too crowded, for the pleasure of nothing at all.

That night, all the empty spaces were filled—with a body or its shadow, a chair brought from his kitchen or elsewhere, an end table yanked out of place to support a drink, a smeared plate, a cigarette in an improvised ashtray. And then there were Hope's things, a shawl over the couch back, fat plush throw pillows, a frowzy ficus abandoned in a corner.

George stood to greet me, followed by Hope. He took my right hand in both of his, and she laid the full flat of her hand on my shoulder; their manner was warm and yet still charged with the party. Hope's hair had begun to come undone in a few tendrils, and her eyeliner had begun to blur. It looked as if she'd been cleaning dishes or making love, and George's face shined with sentiment. I might have been a long-lost someone, or if they were a couple rather than friends, I might have been the person who introduced them. George took the champagne from me and then showed it to his guests—"A classic," he announced. "Ahhh," one or two faces replied. In the half-light I made out a lean middle-aged woman with black hair, black kohl around her eyes, and layers of black lace riding down her body. Her look was Castilian and a touch goth; it was old-fashioned but severe enough to be modern. In any light I could see her skin was so white it hinted at blues. Then there was a trio of men—two a couple, dressed similarly, muscled similarly, and one lone man—short and rounded but distinguished by way of the gray in his neat hair and the crispness of his clothes; his face was as mobile as a clown's. This man said of my gift champagne, translating its name, "The widow . . . People love her."

"I have always liked it," I ventured, forgetting to smile.

"What's not to like," he said, though his tone argued with his words.

"This is Darren," said George. "An old friend of mine. Don't mind him. He's been drinking."

"And smoking—" Darren held up a joint. "And I have enough for everyone."

"This is my landlady, Celia." The couple looked at one another with mirth as if Darren had been caught in a faux pas. Landlady meant officialdom to many. I might wag my head or explain the fire code, but instead, I said, "Darren's very generous," and smiled.

"George will open that and you'll sit by me." Hope took my hand. I let her. The party had grown into its own small knot of confidences, and I was a disruption. Not a fatal one but one that required more cordial interest than the hour of the party provided for. Hope was keeping me safe until I settled into the room with them.

I whispered, "I can't stay."

She whispered back, "Nonsense."

I was parked in a wingchair; I did not recognize it; Hope sat upright in a kitchen chair. Her posture did not look inconvenienced by it. In fact it must be said she had admirable posture.

"I am Josephina." The dark-haired woman leaned in to shake my hand.

Hope explained, "Josephina taught Spanish at St. Ann's for a little while. To my daughter. I taught art, not there, before the kids, at——"

"Not for me, that place," Josephina declared. "So full of effort, to be special, to be more special. Even the parents compete for notice. They hold up their children like mirrors." She threw her chin toward me, pursed her lips, a pantomime of exasperation. Short-lived. Her accent was Spanish. Madrid maybe, but then I was no judge of these things.

"Hey, I was one of those parents," said Hope.

"You do not belong to them. You know that." Then to

me, Josephina explained, "Before you came, we were discussing who we'd like to fuck. I mean people who we are not able to." This was matter-of-fact, languid, not a dare. "I thought of Clive Owen, but I'd have to tie him down. I think maybe he is wild."

"He's no bottom!" squealed Darren. His volume jolted everyone and the place they'd agreed to be—subdued mostly. He adjusted as he lit his joint, and I wondered how I might explain a sudden departure. A sick tenant? Another engagement? All I knew was that I couldn't stay.

"What I mean is that I don't think he'd consent." He dragged in and dragged in, squinting like he was playing cowboy. As he held it, he half-stood and reached from his spot on the corner of the couch clear across the coffee table, over a disorder of cheese and bread, to me. He exhaled his smoke in my direction. "You?" This seemed at once an offer of the joint and a query about this Clive Owen, an actor, but I could not place his face. Darren maintained his position. This was a dare. He wouldn't retreat. Was he affronted by my presence so late in their evening or was he the sort who had to test everyone he met? Who had to be coaxed from his derision?

I didn't intend to smoke, but I reached for the joint—I could not give him the satisfaction of my being demure or awkward. A woman like me does not have to suffer fools at all. Not anymore. But before I could take it, Hope grabbed for it. "I am a woman on the edge. Let me, Darren.

Don't you all know that you are supposed to treat me as if I'm newly widowed? As if I've been shipwrecked?"

I did not pause to consider if Hope knew I was a widow or not; what she said and did right then was about altruism. She'd seen me hesitate.

"Ahhhh, he'll have his young wine," said Josephina. "He'll get drunk on it until he is sick and sorry and come back for you. On his knees. A beggar."

"If you'll have him," said Darren crisply. "I say you move on. He's an embarrassment. I mean that's one tiresome trope. Like his twenty-something bag of flesh is different from all the others."

Hope gave a version of a laugh. "Do women who have been married for twenty-five years move on? Where do we go?" She stared into the smoke for a minute. No one hurried her. "Cary Grant is dead, isn't he?"

"He's beyond dead," intoned Darren.

"I've thought about taking Eva Marie Saint's place on that train at the end of *North by Northwest*. I'd slide right in." She extended the joint to Josephina, bypassing me.

"Darren's pot gives me migraines." Josephina grimaced.

"Everything gives you migraines," he said.

"Oh, my little prick Darren."

"Cunty Joe."

Josephina laughed open-mouthed at this and took a small puff.

"I go back and forth about Cary." Darren straightened

his posture and his tone. He could change on a dime. "I mean, would he be something in bed or too controlled? Could he abandon himself? The guy was some low-budget trapeze artist before he became a studio prize. He's a con man, really, so it would *have* to be performance. He probably didn't know the difference."

"But isn't that what we all want?" asked one of the two men.

"That's Blake," Hope whispered to me. "He runs a gallery I can't resist. And his partner beside him is Andrew."

"I mean if you're good at the performance, if it's seamless, if you're that confident?" Blake asked.

"Well," Hope said, her voice sad, but it rallied, "if he was with one of those starlets, they'd both be performing, right? It would be sexy to watch, surely, but I can't say whether it would be sexy to experience. They'd persuade each other to their fine looks and fine lines, but would they—"

"Inevitably," said Josephina.

"Really? Why?"

"They'd believe it. That's how good they are. As actors. So they believe. And bodies, after all," she said, running her fingers along the white inside of her arm, "aren't hard to fool."

"And you, Celia?" Darren asked.

Among the things my mother and I enjoyed doing together was watching old films; VCR double classics, *His Girl Friday, The Philadelphia Story, The Awful Truth, Notorious*; scenes replayed; tears on tissues, vivid applause. I didn't feel compelled to see contemporary stuff much anymore; it all felt recycled, dull. I said, "He let himself be wild, uncontrolled in his roles. Ugly . . ." I looked at Darren. "Sometimes. He had to be drawing from his own experience, his authority, passions—that's a private place or it should be."

Hope said, "I hope you're right. That's a better way to think of it, him, anybody. That we conserve our private places . . ."

Darren raised an eyebrow. "But that kind of acting is really about control. Maybe the question is just subjective—how sexy is control?"

At that George returned to us carrying the champagne and several flutes. "Sorry. I had to wash some glasses."

"Would you sleep with Cary Grant, darling?" Josephina queried. "That is what we're talking about now, if he would be good in bed."

"What a question. *Of course* I would, if he'd have me. I know there were rumors about him and a cowboy or two, but to me he's so marvelously hetero."

"Was," said Hope.

"We can't let a little thing like that stand in our way," said Darren.

"Death?" I asked gently.

"I meant to be gay or not, but I'd like to believe it's *all* negotiable, dead or alive," Darren laughed, delighted with himself. "Wouldn't you?" He looked at me as if he knew things about me he couldn't possibly know.

"What did Byron say?" George began filling glasses. " 'I

am acquainted with no immaterial sensuality so delightful as good acting.' "

"I remember something Ethel Barrymore said about actresses," said Andrew. "For an actress to be a success, she must have the face of Venus, I think it is, the brains of Minerva, the figure of Juno, the memory of . . . well, a good memory anyway, and the hide of a rhinoceros."

"All that could be said about what it is you need to be a wife. Or the rhino hide anyway." Hope reached for the champagne. She looked into her glass. "I'm not sure how tough I am."

"You're a goddess," said Darren and mooned at her like a boy mooning at the figure of his mother. He loved Hope. He loved her terribly. It wasn't romantic necessarily but it was consuming.

"I am not. I'm a relic."

It was the champagne maybe or my proximity to her, her height, her fine profile, her strong shoulders, her sorrow holding her up, but from nowhere I recognized in me came this statement, which was true enough, true enough to say without thinking: "You're *beautiful*."

Darren regarded me with some alarm at that, and I finally saw to the source of his grief. He wanted no further competition than he already had to be Hope's pet and then I arrived, late, another body, another appetite to navigate. It was time for me to go at last. I'd done what I'd come to do. I stood, which George took as some sort of cue:

"Let's toast to Hope's beauty," he said, standing as well.

Everyone followed suit but Hope.

"Please. Let's not," she said and covered her eyes.

"We can do this without you just fine, dear." Josephina lifted her glass, but before she could proceed, George tried, "Here's to days of new hope."

She conceded, "Okay. I'll drink to that, for everyone."

"New hope for everyone!" cried Darren.

"And here's to George's great adventure," said Blake.

Bon voyages were offered. Wishes of luck. Thanks to the hosts for the excellent food and drink. To George for his generosity. This cheering had voice for long enough that we finished my bottle and another. George went for one more. And before I could interrupt to make my good-byes, it began again: "Come back with a frog in your throat!" called Darren. Then came: "To mind-blowing sex—with frogs!" "To blowing Cary Grant!" "To the lamb slaughtered for our feast!" "May you die in bed at ninety-five years, shot by a jealous lover—or a frog!" Darren drooled, he laughed so. Backs were slapped; arms were raised in mock triumph. Darren waltzed briefly with Andrew, then Blake; he hugged Josephina and then Hope, and she squeezed my wrist twice, conveying something like "isn't this fun?" or "isn't he something?" I did not return the gesture or gestures, though I allowed myself to be brought in. I toasted new friends as preface to announcing my departure. At that, Blake kissed me lavishly on both cheeks and sang out, "Hoopla, Madame! Hoopla!" He smelled of sandalwood and vanilla, and his face was moist and cool and clean and so close, so close. Having emptied another bottle, George went off for more. I felt light-headed and, upon hearing there was no more champagne, slumped as gratefully as everyone else for a seat.

"No toasts without bubbles," pronounced Josephina.

"I have seltzer," George called from the kitchen.

"*Quelle horreur!*" cried Darren.

"Well, then, let's drink this Sancerre. Give me your glasses." George poured, Andrew went to put on more music, and Darren lit another joint. He handed it my way first again. The look on his face was querying and sweet. The man had drooled in front of me. This time I thought he was asking for acceptance, that perhaps he had been from the start and I just hadn't seen it. This time I took it. "I've not done this for a long time," I told the room of them. I had miscalculated the rhythm of things. I hadn't been to a gathering like this in years, did not know how many lives a party could have.

Darren leaned over to me and raised his too full glass, spilling some, whispering loudly into my ear, "To the lamb who came to dinner."

I inhaled and held on and did so again and again, through the contours of the room rounding and seeming to breathe with us, through the cushioning of the sound, through Nina Simone's singing *she can't stand it, daddy*, over and over, giving us notes sung for minutes that refused to be anything as brief as minutes, through a piece of Schubert's (a piece from his Impromptus I think I was told twice), that went fast, then slow, loud, then so soft—the piano so restrained, it actually hurt my ribs—and through the smells in the room, of Blake, of Darren's florid supplies of marijuana, of the cheese back in the oven, and especially of Hope. I don't know when he arrived; if it was an hour after I became stoned and solidly, inarguably drunk or if it was a quarter of an hour. But there he was. I believe I had heard knocking, but the room had been shuddering with all variety of percussion, with the bass and drums and the piano, with tapping limbs and voices, with so many different tempos beating and competing around us only to dig us in deeper. But I remember another sound that felt quarrelsome, discordant, and insistent. I was irritated by it—it reminded me I'd stayed much too long—but then it passed. I forgot about it, and then, yes, there he was.

A long, liquid man. Broad-shouldered and thin-hipped. He stood and surveyed all of us, made sure, it seemed then, that we could see him seeing us, each of us. To me, he appeared a terrifying and bitterly handsome giant in an expensive suit, with his hands pushed into his pockets, making his change dance as if he were punishing it. How loud it was, this advertisement of his distance from us or his disapproval or both; but then his eyes were shrouded by his brow in the half-light of that room, and his mouth which may have wished to express something gentle couldn't through a blanketing of hard-looking stubble over a jaw that was long and edged like a spade. When Hope told us, "This is Les. An old friend of mine, a family friend," we all made an effort to cross through the moat of our far-awayness to greet him—certainly George and Josephina did; George got up and extended his hand but was too late. Already this Les, without need of permission, had lifted a chair from the other side of the room and put it next to Hope. As close to her as he could get. His long arm fell over the back of her chair so that it hung near my head, this man's strong hand pretending to be lazy. He said, "Well, this is cozy. You're all launched, huh?"

"We've been having some fun." Hope wanted to be bright, but the pot, the hour, prevented that. I went to get up, but my legs would not cooperate.

"I bet. Who has the weed?"

"I do." Darren's voice cracked. He was outdone in derision, in natural attributes, in daring.

"May I?"

"There's just this left." Darren handed what remained of the joint to Les. Les pulled out his own lighter and set after smoking, his face becoming a frown of distaste, taking it in and in. Getting the job done. Blowing out trees of smoke, making us all his audience. I don't remember if anyone spoke until Hope offered, "Les lived in the same neighborhood as me a hundred years ago, in North Carolina."

Les nodded as he contained another breath.

"I was the older woman."

"Not so much older," he said to her, exhaling.

"He knows my family," she told us.

He moved the hand that hung near me to encircle the back of her neck. "Do you have a roach clip?" he put to Darren.

Darren nodded, and I saw Hope close her eyes and, with a slight adjustment that I'm not sure anyone saw but me, move herself back and into his hand.

"Youth is willingness," he said to her.

"That," sighed Josephina smiling, "is well said. Do you want some wine?" She was listless, but there was something else in her voice, too, a bluntness to match or impress his.

"Scotch?" he asked her.

"I'll go," said George. "Ice?"

"Sure. Thank you."

"This is the place I'll be staying from now on. This is George's place." Hope went through all our names. When George returned with the scotch, Les said, "Nice place, George."

"Celia here, beside me, is his landlady."

He leaned forward to look at me. He did not remove his hand from Hope's neck. "Nice place, Celia landlady." His eyes stared; they were deeply set and light-colored, maybe green, blue, and were lively until they became bored. Quickly. Obdurate.

"Help me drink this," he said to Hope.

"I couldn't. We've had so much wine."

"Help," he breathed at her, "huh?" putting the glass to her lips, making the ice dance for her. We all waited to see what she would do. Nothing happened for a beat, and then with one hand she took the drink, pointed her gaze there, stared at it, and then sipped; while she did this she snaked her other hand into mine on the armrest, as if she needed me to steady her.

"Is that Chivas?" Les asked George.

"It is," George said.

"It's good."

"It is." George's voice was not warm; it was withholding, careful. Either he did not want to spook this man or he did not want to allow himself to be spooked.

"You off on a trip?"

"With any luck," said George.

Hope continued to grip my hand as Les watched her sip his drink then return it to him and watched her do the same again, three or four times. He still kept one hand on her neck. She did not struggle against it once.

Darren asked Les what he did for a living.

"Whatever I have to do," Les laughed, finishing his drink. "Like everyone else."

"Les is in finance. A hedge fund."

"That's high-end gambling. Hardly an everyman's sport." Darren had found some courage, a trace of spirit in that half-dark room.

"Close enough these days," Les said, raising his glass to finish it. "Shall we go, then? Are you ready?" he said to Hope.

"You're leaving?" said Darren.

I held on to her hand with more pressure. I whispered, "You don't have to go."

"It's okay," she whispered back. "He's an old family friend," she added but without any reassurance or life in her voice. "He knew my mother."

She slipped from me easily and announced, "We have some catching up to do, Les and I." She stood, took her coat from the rack. She then went and kissed all of us, even me, on cheeks or foreheads. Solemnly enough, one by one, while Les stood, hands in pockets again, change complaining. "I had such a lovely night," she said as she moved to the door.

"When will you be home?" George chased after her.

"Not tonight," she said quietly, leaning into George's ear. "Don't worry," she whispered, but I believe we all heard it. We had crawled inside her somehow, and we didn't want to go. "I'll see you in the morning. We'll go to the airport together in the afternoon." I do not think she stopped long enough to look him in the eye. She and the tall man had momentum. The door shut behind them. Darren put his face in his hands.

THE PLEASURES
OF FALLING

——

I WOKE TO A CHILL the next day, in my body, in the building.
Spring was coming, but winter hung on through the
night into the morning. I felt the radiator in my bedroom,
and when its heat did not feel emphatic enough, I pulled
my sweater and jeans on, stuck my feet into slippers, and
went to check the boiler. The quiet in the building was total, the stillness as full as it could be with me there as witness, so I stood in it, with it, in the empty hallway, and felt
the radiator there. It was warm too, but not what I wanted,
not enough. I could smell the party on my sweater—food
and smoke and other people—and then my own smell,
from last night, in my hair, on my body, me having abandoned caution, in increments. I could not say if I was glad,

nor could I explain the goose bumps breaking over me, retreating then returning. Steam heat was expensive, but replacing the system I had with hot water seemed too extravagant when I was renovating. I had regretted the decision here and there since. Steam worked fine, though it had to cycle more to get the job done.

Once down in the basement, I saw that the old boiler, a thrumming centrifuge, was doing what it always did for me, behaving in the expected way.

I did not return to my bed right away. In the hall again, I couldn't yet face the sheets and covers thrown to one side, open and losing heat. In increments. Last night Hope's hand had been so hot in mine; it had begun to burn with that man beside us, his enormous hand collaring her neck. At first I had felt the structure of her there, the light length of the bones of her fingers, the width of her palm; but with her temperature changing so, the flesh overwhelmed the rest; it was what communicated to me; even stoned, drunk, I could feel it, but I couldn't have asked her to stay with us. Who was I? It wasn't my place. I shouldn't even have been there, but it was mine to feel the chill left when her hand was gone and my hand was made a vacancy, something that had to cool and keep cooling. And it wasn't my place to explain to her that when someone is falling, when someone is startled with pain, it is surely better to have someone there who will steady rather than destabilize you or teach you the pleasures of falling.

I knew something about this, sorrow's peculiar altitude

and how disorienting it could be; how the descent into it, through it, can go on and on. You'll grab for anything. The day my husband died, all I could feel was absence, his and my own. I held on to him until he became something other than he had been, and then I could not sit still, but neither could I clean or make phone calls. So I rode the subway. I waited for his body to be covered and removed, signed the papers given me, splashed water on my face, and then I got on the R train at the Court Street stop on Montague Street in Brooklyn Heights, where my husband and I lived at the time. I rode it through rush hour to its terminus at one end in Queens and then to the other, back in Bay Ridge. I did this at least twice. The R was a local, in no hurry; that suited me until I got off at Times Square to transfer to the 2 train. I had thought I might take this back home, but home wasn't home anymore—and I wasn't who I had been even that morning—so impulse dictated that I take it north, all the way above ground to its terminus in the Bronx, which looked more suburban than urban, with more sky than neon.

I had never been to any of these subway line ends; never seen the train pause and seem to take a breath and sometimes admit a new conductor before it went back the way it came. It was nearly evening when I started riding, but bright—it was July. I wore a tank top bought in Ogunquit, Maine, that advertised "Vacationland" and some drawstring cotton capris. My hair was not brushed, and if you looked carefully at my clothes you might have seen some discoloration from sweat, coffee, blood, and urine from a catheter bag. I could not remember if I had brushed my teeth. I know I had forgotten to put a bra on. But no one really saw me, and if they did, especially during rush hour, it was not for long. But later when I switched to the F, when there were fewer bodies in the cars, when I guessed it was finally night, toward 10 or 11 P.M., I got looks, sometimes of concern, sometimes of disapproval. I was unkempt; my shirt was thin. The air must have turned cooler outside because the air conditioner stung more, and people now wore light jackets. I don't know when the man in the summer suit got on precisely, somewhere in midtown. At Fiftieth Street, I saw he was eyeing me. It was around midnight, I think, and I do not know what he saw; I looked back a couple of times to try to ascertain that until he began his approach to me. He was a pink, fleshy man in a wrinkled khaki suit a size too small for him. He was not yet forty, but then with his wrists and ankles sticking out from his suit, with cheeks that looked freshly slapped, and thin streaky blond hair worn too long and made, with gel, to tuck behind his pink ears, he must have appeared younger than he was. I remember when we got off the train together I was surprised by how tall he was and by how his excitement made him sneer. He had moved his seat four times until he was next to me and breathing in my ear, telling me what to do. Did he take courage from the state of me? Yes, I imagine he did. All it took was the pressure of his hand on my lower back to direct me. I had nowhere else to go.

ONE WORLD SEPARATING
ITSELF FROM ANOTHER

———

MONDAY MORNINGS: AFTER THE FORMLESSNESS of Sundays, there was purpose in them. Merciful purpose.

Marina was due that day to clean, to vacuum and mop the hall floors, to dust the sconces and the ribs of the radiators. If she wasn't there by 7:30, she wasn't coming. I never thought of firing her when she didn't show. She and her husband and son had helped to renovate my building, taught me how to plaster, drywall. She'd bring me Ukrainian sausage every so often, not to flatter me but because, she said, "It is good." And I liked how she cleaned when she came, alone or with her son. She talked very little and gave her whole body to the cleaning. She took off her stockings, tied back her hair without need of a mirror, and got down on hands and knees when addressing the floors; she stretched, grunted; her sweat made long oval shapes under her arms and on her chest and stomach. There was no cheer in her movements but such focus and resignation, accompanied by sighs, the voluptuous, well-earned kind.

She did not quarrel with the dirt or the effort it required of her. Her twenty-something son had the same manner, despite his age. He had temperate eyes and a musician's hands. Marina never apologized for not showing. I respected that as well. Women say sorry too often. We say it when it's not ours to say.

On the days Marina was absent, I took some solace in playing her part, a woman with so much history, her own, yes, and her country's, a place that I knew had been pris oner so many times, unlucky in its geography. Once or twice a month I found myself on hands and knees in an old denim skirt. Yesterday in the late morning, George had knocked on my door. He was pressed and nervous and so he whispered with last night's party and that morning's coffee on his breath, a slight hiss to his thank you, his *see you soon,* and then: "Watch after her, will you?"

"Hope? She has so many friends, George. She doesn't need me interfering——"

"She needs everything," he breathed and caught my hand. His was damp with perspiration. "She's not— She's not herself."

"I'll do what I can. Of course."

That seemed to comfort him. Not me, even as he hugged me to the lapel of his jacket, where cologne had newly settled and made the fabric sharp. So I plunged my hands into Monday's soapy water and moved as deliberately as Marina might, rags under my knees, one wet in my hand, which found her rounded strokes, repeated as much for rhythm as thoroughness. Today maybe Marina could not bear the closeness of the subway. Or maybe she wanted to smoke the day away or sit with her son and play cards until he had to go to class or another job. What freedom there was in defection.

It was still early when I completed the top floor—I heard nothing from behind Mr. Coughlan's door. Most likely he was up and gone early, stalking the streets.

On the landing of the floor below were the raised voices of the Braunsteins. The conversation was not yet a fight, but even through their closed door, I could hear it was reaching for one. I'd caught bits of this debate between them before. Words were at odds: "Ready" competed with "not ready"; there was the blocking reply, "When, then, when, damn it?" and something about overpopulation and resources that was countered with "But what will change?" Or "What can?"

I was dug in not far from their door, making it too easy to hear: "Why can't it be about us for a change? Not *them,* Jesus, Angie. Is there no *here* here? Right here and now? You and me?"

Angie was Mitchell's wife. She was a crusader and

Mitchell tried to keep up with her. They participated in candlelight vigils, opposed the death penalty, animal testing, eating veal. She hated Republicans, SUVs, illiteracy, and bleach products. Mitchell loved her. But that morning loving Angie might just have meant hating her. I wondered when it would be too much for him—the chase.

Mitchell threw open the door, exasperated at it and then at the sight of me. His thinness was what you noticed first. He jogged hard every day no matter the weather. His head with its regular spare features and bright gray eyes looked a WASP's but was Jewish in part or whole; situated on top of all that exposed sinew and circulation, it appeared too heavy for him. He tried to contain his annoyance, but he had nothing to hide it behind, no cheeks to speak of, no heavy brows, no excess flesh at all. Not even his clothes were of help: He was dressed for a run in a suit of shining, closely fitting black-and-orange synthetics. I could see his ribs expanding and contracting.

"Celia," he said. A statement.

"Mitchell."

"Celia? Is she out there?" Angie insinuated herself alongside her husband. The top of her head level with his shoulder, she was a short, big-bosomed creature. She was Mitchell's fullness. Or his longing for some. In its motions, her face was passionately earnest—her eyebrows always traveling up with her curiosity, or down, often with disapprobation, her nostrils fluttering; yes, you'd find her too intense, if not for the mole. It was grape-colored and roughly nickel-sized and situated right where a dimple would be. She wouldn't like to hear it gave her a sweet and comic quality. She wouldn't like to hear she looked like a doll. Yellow-haired. Rosy-cheeked. Given to florid blushing or so I imagined. I'd never actually seen her blush, but she slipped their rent under my door every first of the month along with a crisp pamphlet. The latest was about raising the minimum wage.

"No Marina today?" Angie asked. Quarreling enlivened her. The color in her face was higher than ever and there was excitement in her voice. She wore baby-blue cotton pajamas. "I heard a party night before last, didn't I? That wasn't you, was it, Celia?" There was that curiosity, that rigorous hopefulness.

"No, no. George? From downstairs? He's going on sabbatical. I meant to tell you both. I'm allowing him to sublet. As a lark."

"Yes," Mitchell said grimly. "He told me."

"He didn't tell me," Angie said, and to her husband: "You didn't."

Mitchell worked the muscles of his jaw faster and faster, gaining toward something—yelling or bolting or both. I thought it would be good to draw their attention to me.

"You both know I look to maintain a consonance of characters, some harmony . . ." As I went on with an abridged version of the speech I'd given George and Hope, though with none of the same resolve, Angie wrapped her plump arm around her husband's tiny waist. He tried to wriggle it off, but she wouldn't let go. ". . . But Hope seemed a good temporary guest . . ."

They didn't hear me; he tried to remove her arm with his hand; she wouldn't budge. I coughed then, like I had something caught in my throat. "Oh, dear. Excuse me."

"Need water?" Angie asked.

"No, thank you." I had work to do.

"I'm late," Mitchell said.

"Come back in here for a moment, honey. Just for a sec. Okay? Okay."

Had I not been there, I doubt he would have cooperated.

Their door shut and locked. A resolute sound—of one world effectively separating itself from another. I worked over the spot on which Mitchell had just been standing. I heard Angie say, "Sweetheart, sweetheart, *c'mon*." She was probably up on her toes, trying to get to him. Didn't they know fighting about whether to have a child was a luxury?

Not long after moving in, she had painted every room in their apartment, even the short entry hall they stood in now and the bathroom, a different color. She'd asked permission. I didn't think to say no. She opted for pale violet and jade green and a Provence yellow and something like amber, though muddier—a jumble of moods, anticipations, feints. A luxury also.

I was dusting the stair railings when Mitchell flew past, grunting something at me.

I forgot him as I wiped each step a smooth new face on my way down to the next floor, George's, and once there,

I set my supplies to one side, out of the way, to go outside as Marina would—she took cigarette breaks when it moved her. I didn't smoke, but I could take the excuse a smoker might to be still and alone, feel the fresh air for a minute before I completed my work. I must say as I dried my hands on the denim of my skirt and straightened up to go, the world almost seemed simple and knowable; I allowed myself a breath so deep I felt it in the bottoms of my feet; I breathed it out through my mouth, even my eyes. Perhaps I was smiling; I tasted sweat on my upper lip, and felt the tackiness of Pine-Sol on my hands.

What I saw first was her hair. It had been let loose and looked like it had been laid on, rolled on, tugged at, pushed away from her long neck; hands had been inside it and had left their shape and moisture there. Hope hadn't bothered to tame it, reassembling it into a twist. Her blouse, which had seemed stylish but prim when last I saw it, was unbuttoned to the end of her breastbone under her open raincoat. The skin of her face looked rubbed raw; and alarmed red marks on one side of her neck were purpling already as we stood there, not speaking. Hope knew what I was seeing—must have known—and yet she had no impulse to get away, to hide. She licked her lips. They were pale and dry.

"Hi," she auditioned in a whisper as she held herself there before me.

Maybe she was drunk, but she didn't look it. She looked stunned—and though her regard was vacant, her silence and stillness seemed full of expectancy. Maybe she wanted me to fuss over her or apply querying or disapproving looks. Maybe she needed that. To help her feel real again. She had let a man harm her, and now I had some duty to do or say something. As a woman. Yes, the whole complicated landscape of women's relationships was before us on that landing. How we judge one another or try not to, how we care-take, and how much we believe in similarities between us or refuse to.

"I'm cleaning today."

She looked to my supplies, started a smile and then abandoned it, nodded at me once, opened her mouth to say something and didn't. Nothing.

I saw gray in her hair—on the side that stuck straight out; it looked as if someone had made an example of it. Still she stood there.

"The woman who works for me doesn't show some days," I said.

She blinked.

Then I gambled. I wanted so much to go outside and surely what she most needed was her privacy—some reassurance of her own self-possession. I had needed that once; I'd had a map of bruises on my body once. "You're okay, right?" I could have waited for a reply or just waited longer, but I was impatient. I could have reached for her hand, even if it seemed unnatural, too hastily built a bridge right then. Yes, my tone could have been more querying. Instead I instructed, I told her: "You'll be okay. You're all right. You just need a . . . shower. Coffee. These things are—" *What was I saying?* "—common." I fell too hard on "common." What was I saying? *Common enough?*

This woke her eyes. They squinted at me as if she hadn't really seen me there before, then they watered and the gold inside the blue of them glowed. *She* glowed. I had embarrassed her. She was not all right, emphatically, and seemed too confused to move to her door, George's door. For an instant it appeared she didn't quite know where she was or how she got here until she jabbed her hand into her bag in search of her keys. She turned the pockets of her long raincoat out and then sent her hand diving again until it found its object. Then all of her was in motion, to the ends of her hair. The door was opened and then closed. One world effectively separating itself from another.

FROM ATLANTIC
TO PACIFIC

―――

AFTER THAT, I HEARD LITTLE from Hope, from her feet that should have been walking my ceiling or from any other part of her, for a day. I thought to knock on her door, bring something—what? What did women bring one another these days? Casseroles? Booze? I thought to apologize—for what? For being where I did not belong? Where I had such a poor compass from years of disuse. Instead, I crowded myself into inaction with platitudes, the ones we all barter in, that time heals, that a good night's rest is the stuff, that we're all grown-ups here. I even composed other speeches, practiced divulging something, for her sake, but my tongue only flopped around, incapable. So when the crying came I listened with relief. At first. Was attentive to it out of respect. She hiccupped, working her way in, and then leaned into peals, which said no and please and no again. I found out she had lungs and stamina for this.

It went on for three nights, sometimes during the dinner hour but mostly just after, when the rest of the world had done their washing up and were preparing to go to bed and more often than not into someone's arms. I knew this nowhere time well. She moved from bedroom to living room and back again. When one room was too full of grief, she found the other, to fill it up. She shuffled, walked, bolted. To the bed, then to the hardness of that leather couch, letting it hold her for as long as she could bear it. Last night, she'd gone hoarse yet she stayed at it. Her cries were staccato and pointed and she carried them into both rooms, back and forth, moving slowly, as if spraying the present with the shards of them, trying to break it up. A battery. Steady enough.

My sleep had become fragmented too. I'd lived with sleep deprivation before. I had cried and worked the floors. I had examined my hands that had touched him last and marveled at them. Not here. I hadn't brought that grief with me here or that was my intention. I wanted order for me, the building. I'd wanted certain barriers, the right to them. But sleeplessness makes your days feel rubbery, the walls thin and movable. How much could I have expected from this new place once I'd filled it with people? And in a building that had already been stretched and reimagined by locals so many times?

I took some refuge in its history—that long before I was born or dreamt of the building that I would own, it had been classified as a brownstone once, or so the record keepers indicated, but when the city bureaucracy was a network of cronies with itchy palms someone had looked the other way and its conversion began. Before there was a landmark preservation committee, before Robert Moses tried to raze much of downtown Brooklyn in favor of an expressway, the grand front stairs were disassembled and taken away. Fireplaces were closed up and what remained of them was encased in the walls. Stained glass was carted off.

It must have taken more than a few pairs of hands to accomplish the theft—and so conspiracy—to strip this building of mine and make it something other than it was intended to be. In modern-day parlance, it became a walk-up and then came the complication of the elevator. No one had approved its installation, though someone, his pockets full, had known of it because then the official designation of the building changed to apartment building. Stolid. I could not restore all the Italianate touches that had been sanded down or removed. I did my best by the ceiling moldings that remained, by the floors, the light fixtures, the banisters. What I could not restore, I replicated; what I could not replicate, I left simple but clean. I could feel the bones of the place—that I'd fortified them. And me. But now Hope rattled them through the night, and my head was not clear.

When the heat cycled on at 6, I was awake to hear it. Outside, birds complained of what continued to be a cold March—as the light gained, they did too in their fussing and calling and bickering. Still, my ears picked out Mr. Coughlan's approach. He was not a heavy man, but as he went up or down the stairs, it was never hard to make out his reckoning with what it was to convey his body around now and the care he assigned to every step.

Soon after came Mitchell Braunstein's feet. The soles of his sneakers barely landing on the wood. He bounced down, leaving little evidence of himself behind him, already envisioning himself moving with the morning on the other side of the door, and full of the sort of energy that shamed me sometimes.

I struggled to drag myself vertical, telling myself that the early light is so often the answer to confusion.

I'd had to visit a sleep clinic; in my first year alone, when insomnia had become a constant, and I could not keep from remembering for fear I'd forget. Evidently I had to reteach my body what time it was, reset its clock. If we let them be, our bodies can be simple mechanisms, as responsive to light and dark as tulips. Did Hope know this? To force herself into the light for at least twenty minutes every morning? How essential routine was to keep us upright? I listened for her as I forced a cup of black tea down, made myself as presentable as I could in a light coat and jeans, and still I listened for her and could not find the door. It was my habit to go out just before or after rush hour. I hesitated and as I did was put in mind of a woman, a stranger to me, who announced she'd never sleep again. "It's not safe," she explained.

Yes, it was years ago, before I bought my building, when I was still not my own entirely. I'd been tricked into attending a support group for the recently bereaved by my well-meaning sister-in-law, Maureen. A newly minted trauma counselor, she came to the city from Boston often after 9/11, to suss out the varieties and degrees of trauma felt by her even in the sidewalks. She wanted to put her face into the epicenter of it, taste the mess of it. I did not, or not more than living here required of me or anyone. But would I come and observe her conducting a group therapy session? Give her feedback? Meet some like-minded women? Who else could she count on? I didn't have it in me to say no. Not then. She'd been suspicious of me, maybe she was yet. He hadn't wanted to die in hospice, and I defended that choice as if I were defending his life, rather than his death. And just when I might have listened to reason, to Maureen, and handed him over to steadier hands, he had died suddenly. Or not suddenly.

No, it was a lifetime in that room. When I did manage to sleep then, I could feel myself slipping back into that room, counting his breaths. Alone with him again. And even if I told myself it was his choice, I had done it: deprived Maureen a place there.

So I watched as the women—it was a women's group—formed a circle; I remember being amazed that they could keep their seats even as rage choked the air around them.

One woman reported her husband had worn dirty underwear that September day. They'd been too busy for laundry. Another that her husband had eaten his favorite breakfast that morning. Maple-flavored oatmeal a consolation to her even still. When someone asked me to share, mistaking me for one of them, I told them out of politeness, with Maureen nodding her encouragement, that my husband was gone over a year ago by way of a protracted illness. Each in their different way looked at me as if I'd betrayed them, and I hated Maureen then as I did when she had insisted he die in a hospice and I denied her every entreaty, no matter how polite, or when she called wanting to talk about her brother since then—to catalog his habits, his affections, the set of his eyes. Yes, I'd say, his eyes were brown; yes, he loved music, books, the northern Atlantic coast, but I would not give her Coltrane, Bowie, Bill Withers, or Coney Island in high season or York Beach, Maine, just after the tourists left in the fall or how he smelled of summer all year round and loved Melville for his recklessness and made me love him, too, or that I'd read Proust and Jane Austen to him even while he rolled his eyes at me, pretending he didn't like it, testing my commitment, touching me in places I liked to be touched to distract me. Because he could quote from *Moby-Dick* I came to as well. I didn't anymore or only rarely, though I kept copies on hand, within reach to test my memory. . . .

I did not talk of my husband. People wanted details. I had millions more, and they were greedy for them, for news of a love I still observed, but something hard and visceral in me refused to give it. He belonged to me alone. That was the price of his leaving me as he did, when he did. Privacy is not something Americans understand well anymore: You are only as real or worthwhile as the stories you surrender and even then, even if you're willing, there's no guarantee you'll pass. Especially with women my age, any age, really, who too often trafficked in feelings for leverage. You see, I didn't want these sorts of tests to factor into my days. I did not care for expectations now. I couldn't afford to.

Years ago, I read a review of a reissue of a book by a German writer, Peter Handke. It was a memoir about his mother and her suicide. The reviewer, a novelist, wrote that Handke's mother's sort of death didn't rank as much of a tragedy in the scheme of things, in the face of mass murder, genocide, famine. One aging middle-class woman taking her life was prosaic. Too small. And the widows in that support group probably would have agreed, that certain griefs trump others. But they did not know my husband, what I lost, or what I had done, and I could not, would not, tell them.

Upstairs came a clatter, a pot or pan hitting the floor, the metal reverberating. Hope did not rush to collect it. Likely she was watching it try to settle. When it did, when I heard nothing more for a space of a few minutes, I made it to the door, and out of the building. There were the birds again—so loud with their business that for a moment I thought the world was theirs, but then with the chilled air finding its way through my clothes, I had to walk, and there on the corner I saw the cars and taxis and delivery trucks climbing Clinton Street; they were panting and hollering, brakes trilling, overwhelming the birds.

And on the sidewalks came the first wave of the morning's rush-hour pedestrians. I remembered what it was like, the competition with the lights, the awareness of the clock in every part of your body, and all the calculations going in your head despite you. Brooklyn Heights, Cobble Hill, Boerum Hill, Carroll Gardens, all of downtown Brooklyn into Park Slope was populated by variations of middle class, from low to high. The neighborhoods had become so desirable, for the proximity to Manhattan and the prettiness of the streets, the quality of the schools, that people did what they had to to stay, and, more, to belong; they paid in iPods, iPhones, and BlackBerrys, in fashionable shoes, handbags, and jobs, with the highlights in their hair, the cut of their dresses and suits and pants, the contributions to the Botanic Garden, Housing Works, NPR, and Doctors Without Borders. Never mind the rents, the condo and parking fees. I could almost hear the arithmetic that meant more tender considerations were left behind, that got them to the subway and into their offices.

But I could stroll. I could walk away from the subways

on Montague Street, and as I turned to do so I saw a young woman walking toward me, marching really, shoulders up by her ears, face a knot, math going. How much time, how many blocks, when could she afford a building with a doorman, laundry, a view? Not yet. She was not many years out of college. She'd foregone stockings and her legs under her skirt were pink with the cold, though she would not concede to it. Spring meant no stockings. She gripped a magazine in one hand like she might hit someone with it and glanced at me dismissively. Hadn't I somewhere to go? For as long as our eyes met I knew a moment's panic. And with guilt I thought of my own bills. I had a new roof to put on the building. I could afford it. Over time. Yes. There was time.

I watched her as she crossed Atlantic Avenue into Brooklyn Heights, where I used to live with my husband. I had considered moving farther away but only made it to the other side of Atlantic. To Pacific Street. From Atlantic to Pacific, no real distance at all.

I almost didn't see Mitchell Braunstein making his way down the street. Even from two blocks and some away, I could observe how he had challenged his leanness. His head and arms, hanging, looked carelessly attached; his steps were smaller than usual for a man of his height, six feet or so. I do not know how far he'd run, but it looked as though he'd gone full out and was accounting for it now. He hadn't seen me yet, and before I could decide to avoid greeting him or not, he appeared to remember something;

he looked stricken with the remembering and went back in the direction he'd come. It was his urgency that made me follow him. Perhaps he'd dropped his key or his wallet. Perhaps I could help. Landlords had some obligations, and my head was not clear.

He walked quickly and so did I. When he broke into a trot, I did the same. Then he halted just short of Atlantic Avenue, as if he'd run into something or someone. His body reared up slightly. He paced, appeared to catch his breath, then bent to put his hands on his knees, his elbows making dangerous angles for anyone who came too close. His head lowered again. It looked like he might let it fall at last, let it go, that great heavy head of his, and just when I thought so, thought I should turn back before he saw me seeing him, turn into the tide of commuters who did not have time to take Mitchell or me in, he set off again. This time, thankfully, he simply walked at a pitch. One I could match, at a remove.

He led me across Atlantic. I could not pass from Cobble Hill into the Heights without feeling a slippage, sometimes light, sometimes severe, into the past. I did not do it often. But if I kept my focus on him, on what was new, the new chill, the forsythia with its whiplike limbs tipping a new yellow, trying to bloom despite the cold, I could navigate it, yes, with Mitchell, my tenant of over four years, on Henry Street, turning on Montague, past the used bookstore from which my husband and I had taken home so many books, past the Polish diner where we ate boiled pierogi and suffered the indifference of the bored Polish waitstaff, to the Promenade.

It was cantilevered above the Brooklyn–Queens Expressway, which, along with all the city streets, fumed with the new day's exhaust, its noise and ambition, but Mitchell never minded this or the view of the harbor and lower Manhattan, as if he had no room for any of it now, as if he had no past or future. It was lovely to witness, this race of his, until he found his object, sitting in the middle of the line of benches. He stopped to see her fully first and so did I. A woman who was as lean as he, nearly as tall, as poured out from exertion, in her running clothes, her nose and cheeks ruddied; her damp dark hair seeping out from an unremarkable woolen cap to her jawline. Before I could properly size her up, decide if she was merely a sister or a running friend from work or college with whom he'd just quarreled maybe, he wrapped himself around her and she curled into him. They held on as if someone threatened to come and pry them apart. Or as if they were freezing. They hid their faces in the other's dampness, what had to be a cold damp now. Salty. They did not see me. How could they? A woman standing where she did not belong.

TEA AND WHAT
WAS EXPECTED

———

I WOKE LATE, and as the morning became midday I could still inhabit a dream and it me and I could see my husband reaching for me with both arms, but they were black with this new green, inky with it, and he was laughing. The phone rang. I didn't answer it, and when it rang again, this time in a way that struck me as plaintive, I unplugged it. I thought to go back to bed, but I threw water on my face, attended to my teeth, made coffee, still seeing him reaching for me so when the knock came at the door, my door, I could not but think for the interval it took to turn the knob, the lock, that it was him, that he'd managed to find me here. I hadn't gone too far away. I'd stayed just close enough, on the other side of Atlantic. But a young man presented himself instead. Hope's son. Unmistakably. The one I'd seen pulled into her on the street once months and months ago.

"Hello," he said. "Good morning." Measured. Almost decorous. Had he been taught not to fidget or was it his nature to stand so still?

I caught myself staring, said hello back.

"My mother, upstairs?"

"Yes, oh, yes, is everything okay?"

He paused to consider that. Oak and sand winding through his brown hair. Eyes like his mother's, though darker overall as if someone had thrown in bits of peat. And so solidly made through his trunk and well-formed limbs. Young, yes, but a man already in body.

"With the apartment?" I clarified.

"Yes, fine, or I think so." A dazed something in his manner caused him to pause again. "Thanks, I mean for the apartment. Thanks for the apartment." There was a scent of pennies, of copper, coming from him and something cedary in his sweat. He rolled forward on the balls of his feet, then stopped, catching himself.

"You're welcome. I'm sorry, I didn't get your name."

"Sorry, yes, I'm Leo."

"I'm Celia."

"She told me. The landlady."

"Yep."

"My mother wants me to invite you to coffee, no, tea, that was it, tea with us, upstairs. With my sister and me.

So we can meet you. She'd like that. In about an hour?"
He was not used to being her emissary, or not in years, but
he wouldn't think of turning her down now. When I hesitated, he pursued me, for her. "Just for a minute. She has
her mind set on it." He did not resort to charm, as she did.
He looked down as he reported, "She's singing," and then
surprised me by looking at me directly. It woke me—that
sincerity. There it was again, and with her eyes reimagined on him. I did not know how to reply except the way
he most wanted. "Okay. In about an hour then."

I thought I could manage it—do whatever was expected
for an hour. I thought I was sufficiently alert when the
door to George's apartment opened and Hope's daughter
smiled through puffy eyes and blotched cheeks, threw
her shoulders back and gave me a long neck, her mother's,
yes, a display of poise and simple courtesy.

I don't know what I saw first once the girl moved off
and let me in—that the place had now settled into a soft
overgrowth, of flowers, some expensively arranged, some
carelessly, and of more bright pillows and afghans, one
hooked over the couch, another on the wingchair, another
folded on a footstool I had never noticed before.

It was as if Hope was primed to put on an extended
slumber party—something green, a soft something for
the head, a coverlet reckoned for each potential guest. She
or her children had also managed to displace books so that

here and there they leaned into one another on the shelf like school friends or were littered around the room, a few abandoned mid-read, left wide open. And I smelled gardenias, a scent stronger than any other in that room, than the tea already set out and steaming in a white and rose-stenciled ceramic pot, than the perfumes of mother or daughter or the unmistakable scent of the boy.

The gardenia was my mother's favorite flower and as such had been a burden to me and to my father when he was still alive. Gardenias, being tropical, don't grow in the Northeast save in a hothouse or with concerted effort; and because they bruise easily, die quickly, florists don't always favor them; they can't be relied on to play their part. My father and I often watched Mother's Day corsages, picked up that Sunday morning, turn brown right on my mother's wrist even before the afternoon had fully arrived.

I tried to focus on the girl but found myself scanning for the source of the fragrance—their scent is sweet, thick as musk. The girl said, "I'm Danielle Boxer. My mother has said so many lovely things about you." Her kindness had no body to it. She extended her hand, not to shake, but to introduce me game-show style to the food forming a battalion around the teapot, a pile of enormous scones, fruit, Camembert, a quiche. "We have so much to eat," she declared in a tone that asked "What will we do?" The daughter's large eyes were a diluted blue; they skittered over things, and her skin was milk-pale and so given to showing every emotion, the action of blood in her veins. Her cheeks were fuller than either her mother's or her brother's, yet when she gave me her profile, it was sharp and Roman. She had two faces competing in the one—a girl's and a woman's. When her baby fat burned off in her cheeks (where the last of it remained), she'd be striking in an austere way, but for today, perhaps owing to circumstance, she was plainer and frailer-seeming than her mother. And her outfit—recalling Audrey Hepburn, a high-collared sleeveless blouse with flounced bow and twill gray cropped pants—looked expensive, as formal as mourning clothes, and painfully grown-up.

"Feel free to sit—everyone's here or around here—I mean if you'd like to sit." Danielle said this with a fluttering gaze that expected anarchy or disaster of me, all while her hand kept reaching to ensure her chestnut hair was not escaping the tight ponytail she'd assigned it to.

"Mother," she called to the kitchen, "Your *friend*—"

"Celia," I helped and sat on the edge of the footstool.

"Yes, *Celia* is here."

"Good, good," called Hope. "Be right there."

"Can you believe all these gorgeous books?" the girl asked, though her tone once again betrayed her; it suggested that the books unsettled her. *So many books.*

"George is a reader," I told her.

"A collector. He has Simone de Beauvoir and Colette. A first edition of *The Second Sex*. Yes." She nodded to herself, surveying, blinking, then, "It's a nice apartment," but there was such querying force in this too that I could easily take it to mean she didn't care for the apartment at all or wanted, powerfully, to be elsewhere. Suddenly so did I.

"Here I am." Hope swanned in, hair swept up without one dissenting strand, at once full and contained, lipstick on. She wore a man's white dress shirt, blue trouser pants, and a silk ivory scarf tied around her neck.

"Leo?" she called.

He emerged from the bedroom. "Sorry, I was——"

"Indisposed," his mother supplied.

"Right."

"Celia, welcome."

I stood.

"You met my children."

"Yes," I said softly. "A pleasure."

"Come, everyone, sit. Let's eat. Let's get to know Celia. She's been very generous to me, allowed me to stay at George's."

It was an overstatement, it embarrassed me. Perhaps that was the point of the invite.

A stream of commentary accompanied Hope's movements as she poured tea, offered cream, sugar, honey. "Leo has always loved honey." The scones were almond and cinnamon, respectively. "And Danielle wouldn't eat anything but bread as a baby." Hope did not rush. She'd done this before and did it commandingly. I wanted to ask after the gardenias—I still could not pinpoint their source—but I didn't, relaxing instead into Hope's patter. There was song in her voice and pleasure—the pleasure of being a hostess, mother, of demonstrating this. The marks on her neck were covered by the scarf and may have healed. Whatever their state, this was meant to be a new day. Her skin was unblemished; her eyes were clear. "The tea is called Thé de Fête, party tea. We bought it in Paris at Mariage Frères, this wonderful teahouse in the Marais. You have to go if you haven't been."

"I haven't."

"I took the kids when we'd go every year, but now they're selling tea all over the world and it's lost its specialness a little, hasn't it?"

Danielle nodded at her mother and said vacantly, "Globalization."

"Or progress," said Leo, without contention. "I mean they have a good thing."

"Yes, but that doesn't mean they should just give it away," said Danielle, blinking, "to anyone."

"They're not giving anything away," said Leo calmly.

"We haven't been to Paris this year. The kids' schedules have been harder. Danielle's finishing her senior year. Leo has a job."

"We were there last year," Danielle said. "I studied there. At the Sorbonne. All of us were there . . . All *four* of us."

Hope's back stiffened. "Yes, that's right. Well, Celia, you'll have to tell me if you like the tea—it's got a lot of vanilla in it. Can you smell it?"

Here was my chance. "Yes, now that it's in the cup. It smells delicious, but I keep smelling gardenia. That can't be the tea."

"Oh, no, or yes, it's in the bedroom. An adorable plant with what? Two blossoms?"

"Three," said Danielle.

"A gift from my children."

"Oh, how nice."

"What a scent," Hope marveled. She sipped her tea. "I grew up in North Carolina and under my bedroom window there was this old chicken coop that had been claimed by what I still swear was this wild growth of gardenias."

"You *still* swear?" Danielle asked.

"Oh, well, I've since been told by someone who claims to be an authority on these things that gardenias don't grow wild in North Carolina, that it couldn't have been gardenias or that it's unlikely."

Danielle put her teacup down. "But you've always told us it *was* gardenias, Mother. I mean, that's why we bought the plant for you. To remind you." Color climbed up Danielle's cheeks; her brow broke into lines.

"Well, it might have been. That was the scent or that's what I recall. It was so powerful—"

"How could you get that wrong? I mean how could

someone get that wrong? All these years, you told us that story, since we were little. Gardenias, gardenias and that *seductive* fragrance everywhere, just *everywhere*. That's what you told us. They were there——"

"Danny, it's okay. It was the right thought," Leo put in. "It was Danny's idea." He became still, his head cocked with one ear higher than the other as if he were trying to make out more inviting sounds at some distance.

"I love gardenias, darling. I'm so grateful. Drink your tea before it gets cold. It's your favorite."

"No, this is *Dad*'s favorite." Danielle used both hands to smooth back her hair, once, twice, three times.

"This tea? No, I don't think so."

"Yes, Mother. It is. You couldn't have forgotten already. He'd order this and a——"

"Leave her alone, Danny." Leo strained not to move, to keep his voice level.

"I just mean she should know these things. I do. You do. Daddy does."

"Stop," Leo almost whispered. "It's not her fault."

"I know that." The girl's eyes filled. "Of course. It's that *all* the details are important. It's how we know . . . what matters." The blood took over her face entirely. Her mouth went into a tight, straight line—it was not her mother's mouth; it had none of her fullness. It was prettily formed but thin and in its austerity reminded me of many of the faces of the Connecticut town I'd grown up in. She'd have to earn personality, find some generosity, for a mouth like that, her father's perhaps. She was the only one who'd introduced herself using her last name, his last name.

"Danielle speaks a beautiful French. Eat something, darling. I bet you haven't eaten today. She's been studying a lot for her finals and it's never easy to leave college behind."

Danielle bit into an almond scone. It appeared to disgust her.

"What sort of work do you do, Leo?" I asked.

"I frame pictures."

"He just started that recently. He's very good with his hands. He even designs the frames. He works with artists, galleries."

"My PR agent." He nodded at Hope.

"He *was* in banking," Danielle reported, sullen, chewing still.

"I worked with my dad, but I quit a few months ago."

"He always wanted to try this, right, darling?"

"Right."

"Blake—remember Blake? Who runs the gallery? From George's party? He relies on Leo." Hope aimed high, for buoyancy. "And my father painted, and he built his own frames. Leo comes by it naturally."

"That's great." I slid a grape in my mouth.

"Right," Leo said again.

"I have champagne if anyone wants some," Hope offered. "And shall we have some music? George has all these great compilations." She attended to the stereo, then turned to us. "Everyone try the quiche. I put Gruyère in it. Even if that's sacrilege, to whom? Who can tell me?"

"Julia Child," Danielle recited obediently, trying to recover her mood, though her voice was weary. She nodded at me. "Traditional quiche Lorraine requires no cheese."

"That's right. So I'm transgressing, and I *love* it, love it, love it. Leo, cut everyone a piece for me, will you?" To me she said, "It's a wonder you know the scent of gardenias so well."

"It was a family favorite."

"You've got to see it." Hope retrieved the potted plant. As she did, a man's voice sang "Nobody Knows the Trouble I've Seen" to an up tempo. She held it out in front of her. "Doesn't it take you away, just looking at it?"

The dark shine of its full, dark green leaves, its cream-colored blossoms wide open and pouting extravagantly did belong to another climate where growing and dying happened all at once, in a tumble, where they didn't wait for anything or anyone, let alone for seasons to change or for mourning. Its smell came at us from everywhere, seizing on every particle of the air we took in. I breathed through my mouth and saw that already one of the flowers had begun to curl into itself, turning dingy so quickly.

"That's Sam Cooke singing," said Leo, but neither that fact nor the cheer of the song's arrangement could quite strip the blues from the song; we heard "trouble" over and over; it snapped at us, and in a room so suffocated with so insistent and yet so fragile a fragrance there was nowhere to hide.

Danielle started weeping before Sam Cooke had finished; her posture crumbled and she said, "Oh, Mother, I'm sorry. I'm *so* sorry."

Leo stood up from his hips, without leaning forward, as if he'd grown straight up from the chair, and then held himself there, frozen. I stood too. The boy hung his eyes on mine, didn't blink. If I was invisible to the girl, I was not to him: I did not know whether I was meant to bolster him in some way, or act, if he was imploring me—*do something*. I watched as Hope scooped Danielle into her, and for a moment I was gone, seeing that embrace on the Promenade, Mitchell and that woman, how skin can and can't give way, how you wish it could finally, give way. Hope spoke into her daughter's neck and hair, "It's okay, baby. It's a hard time, but it's okay. I'm here. Mumma's here."

At that, I walked to the gardenia directly, picked it up with both arms. Its foliage pressed into my mouth and nose as I carried it to the door—a green so dense. I put it outside, in a far dark corner of the hall. When I came back, I reported, "It's too strong." I did not say this loudly or wait for a reply. I reached and squeezed the solid width of Leo's forearm once fast so as not to know his skin or temperature too well. I placed my hand on Hope's shoulder as George might, gently, and whispered a thank-you. Then I left Hope to her children.

A MAN VANISHES

———

Two sets of feet stepping with care, as if afraid to agitate too much, over my head. Slippered or socked, padded anyway. March, as it turned into April, kept its bite at night and mother and daughter folded into one another. Two days and nights like this, the two alone, from what I could tell, growing quieter and quieter, as if the absence of noise might mean the absence of pain. The gardenia remained in the hall. I waited for it to die. Perhaps they did, too.

I reconnected my phone. I dialed in for my messages. Marina's voice—heavy in English, revealing little, a flat hello and will you call. *Thank you*. Mr. Coughlan's daughter, her voice as tight as a rusted screw. Two calls from her. The second screechy—*please let me hear from you*. False

graciousness. The roofer wondering if I accepted his esti-
mate: a businessman who knew to speak to me with friendly
reserve, to keep his message short but lively, as if each
word was a firm handshake. *I look forward to hearing back.*

Finally a message from Mitchell's wife, Angie: I could
hear her face opening and closing as she asked if we could
discuss the building's recycling policy again. She believed
the definitions were expanding. She hesitated. "More
plastics . . . Containers." She rarely hesitated.

I tended to the building. I sorted the recycling as I always did, I tied the garbage bags, avoiding expanding definitions for now. I looked to do some weeding in the garden
but was not sure which were the weeds and which weren't.

One afternoon, having slept well, I volunteered as I
sometimes did, several times a month, at Helping Hands,
sifting the donated clothes, shoes, housewares. Then I
walked Cobble Hill—away from Atlantic Avenue. I bought
berries, pasta, tuna fish. I picked up a bottle of whiskey.
Jameson. My husband's brand when he had a taste for whiskey. Before it got too late, I returned the calls made to me
the day before, relieved to get voice mails all around. No
one answered their phone anymore.

I sat and listened for mother and daughter, for a third
night of their sort of quiet. I ate tuna from the can. I let dark
come in the apartment, bend its lines and cool my face.

How long did it take me to form the sounds I began to
hear above me into a scenario? First there was a table
scudding across tile, tile I had installed in George's kitchen.

Then the table, George's exquisite cherry table, finally meeting the wall, hitting it again and again, being made part of a rhythm. Hope's utterances, high and loud enough to reach me, giving volume and consequence to the rhythm; and a man's voice shaping and directing all the noises. What was he saying? I couldn't say, though it was two words. One syllable each. They didn't have to have meaning up there or down here—what they advertised was his control and the pride in it. Her voice went off at longer intervals. Then I heard what seemed like a squeal. I stood. I could remember her son's eyes on mine, the blooming color in his lips and along the edges of his nostrils. I opened the kitchen window for air, without thinking. Doing so brought them closer, with my kitchen right below George's. The same alert night air reaching for them, reached me now. I could hear "please" from her, then the intelligible commentary that spoke of pain and pleasure, and from him, "That's right." Then loud, "Say it." Not a yell exactly but delight in volume, in his freedom with it, with her. "Stay with me, damn it!" Hope falling wholesale into a place where words had no place. The table rocked and then seemed to lift; it barked against the surface and was held there: "Say it or we start all over again. The whole thing."

"Pleeeaaase."

The wall took blows again. And a hand clapped on skin—hers. What else could it be?

Sex could fragment into clichés. But in the acting out

of them they weren't anymore; those familiar positions, roles, words—they became sensation, feeling. A shock of feeling: a slap given was particular to the shape of his hand, its strength, and to where on her body she took the flat of his palm, how welcome it was or wasn't, how much it stung. I had almost forgotten this as I mapped them in my mind—her beneath him, the table digging into her stomach as she gave him the full of her backside and took his weight and its concussions. It hurt, because it always did when you wanted to be no better, no worse, than animals.

I couldn't leave the window when the phone rang, though I imagined yanking it from the wall. Could they hear it? And didn't they imagine I could hear them?

She'd given me a glorious display of her maternal self on Sunday. It seemed to matter I saw it, her fine management of the afternoon, her children: "Mumma's here." That thin scarf around her neck tied so jauntily. And now the colors of Les's voice, dark blues and browns, all hewn marble, and its pace, never hasty. Was it him making me party to this? Or was I simply beside the point? Here, in my own home. They did not know that sound carried so, that the floor that was my ceiling was old and every day more permeable? I shut the window as the telephone stopped ringing, poured myself a tall whiskey in semi-dark that wore too dark suddenly, and turned on all my lights. I left the kitchen but so did they. As I dialed my voice mail to find out who called, thudding followed me. If someone were with me, my husband, we might have laughed at something showier than that gardenia's scent. We might have been able to package all this into commonplace. I would not have worried for her neck or where else he might leave his mark. But alone the noise was everywhere. It was the liveliest thing in my apartment. I had no place to put it. *Uh-uh-uh*. That's what I thought I heard bearing down as Mr. Coughlan's daughter told my voice mail, "He's not answering his phone or the bell. I was there. I tried your bell too. You didn't answer. Have you seen him?" Something fell overhead. A lamp? George's elegant lamp? "Can you tell me if you've seen him lately. *Please*. I'm so worried."

I did not know I was running until I stumbled and felt my heart in my legs and feet too acutely. I gripped his key in my hand like a dagger, as if it had remedy in it already. But when I got to his door, all of me froze. I almost turned around. I studied his door. The imperfections of the paint. I did not paint this door, not this one, others, but I had chosen the color. I touched it. The comfort of wood, the waxiness of high gloss. I knocked carefully. He could be home, just returned, or sleeping, or merely wanting privacy. No one answered the phone anymore. I knocked again. Please, I said to myself while hearing not Jeanie Coughlan, but Hope saying it at the same time, drawing it out as she had, threading it into an evening that was not intended to be my evening. I got angry then, insensibly. I stabbed at the lock, finally working the key in, but of course it was already unlocked. The key was useless. How many times had I spoken to him about this? I was a landlord, not a nurse or a mother-confessor. I was not his daughter.

"Mr. Coughlan?" It took work to hold my voice as low and impersonal as that. "It's Celia, your landlady. Are you here? I've had an inquiry from——"

Darkness as in a cave, silence as absolute, and me diminishing with knowing I had to break it. There was no one here, no one who could or would respond. My hand searched and found the switch for the overhead light. Objects jumped to—his chair, standing lamp, radio, the yellowing charts on the wall, the blue enameled kitchen table to one side, where he took the meals he didn't take in his chair. An arrangement which in its extreme simplicity didn't mean things didn't matter, but that it was just these few that did or should, that chair, that old lamp, that radio, and the path from them to the window. How many times had he walked it to see water? In this bedroom, the double bed on a metal frame had no headboard and no occupant; the sheet and a rough blue blanket had been assembled and pulled smooth. In the bathroom, the single towel was dry. The surfaces had been wiped down lately, if not scrubbed. Two cans of soup were left in his cabinet. In the fridge, the cheese was mostly gone; the bread, of which four slices remained, had begun to mold. Perhaps his eyes couldn't decipher it, flecks as yet. None of this spoke of a hearty appetite, but it did not necessarily speak of illness or precipitous departure either. In the past weeks, Hope's presence had distracted me: I had bought the soup for him, one or two cans at a time so as not to be overly conspicuous; when I could, I'd replace the cheese he'd once picked up, once chosen himself; I'd done so at least a half-dozen times. I always opened it, cut off the hard end. I stuck ten- and twenty-dollar bills in his wallet, once or twice a month—he never remarked the money or the food, or if he did, saw fit not to comment.

It was nearly 10:30. I fell into his chair, a recliner that was mostly wide planes of worn wood save for leather-upholstered padding on its seat and back that had begun to lump and sag to fit the shape of the missing man; the chair's seams were full of crumbs, its smell musty, old, but not unpleasant. I let my lungs fill with it, and with the still-ness that had shocked me when I entered his apartment.

I hadn't noticed till it stopped, but I had been shaking a moment ago, and now I was here, alone, far from everyone else. I was grateful to Mr. Coughlan, yes, wher-ever he was. I'd simply wait for him here. I'd explain the intrusion with worry, his daughter's. By midnight he'd be home surely. Even an old man wasn't immune to the spring air on his skin, under it. He'd be home by midnight surely.

I woke to bare bulbs shining on me—the overhead light I had switched on. Mr. Coughlan had removed the cover, perhaps to change one or both of the bulbs. How bright it was, how sharp, and then came low and high whines, scraping—the rearranging of things, heavy pieces. It sounded like furniture. The Braunsteins underfoot at their own adventures. It was just after midnight. Late for redecorating. I stood and surveyed the place before leaving. The only window he'd left open was the one with the view. On a calm night you could hear the ferries sounding. I heard the roll of wheels outside on the street, a cart or skateboard, the chirping signal of a car locking, and finally with the Braunsteins agitating again, I knew some defeat. I would have to call his daughter first thing. She'd want to call the police and she'd be right to. I in turn would have to talk to my tenants about rules and order, about quiet and prudence.

Turning off his lights, locking two and so all of his locks, I took a right in the short hall outside and tried the door to the storage room beside his apartment; it was the reason his place was smaller than the other units, that and the lower ceilings. Inside, things from a former life. Books, tapes, CDs, old movies: *His Girl Friday, Wings of Desire, Notorious.* Things I could not give away, that I didn't want to risk to dampness in the basement, but that, looked at too often, might become as common to the eyes, and heart, as wallpaper. Then I called for the elevator. If ever I needed to be carried it was now. It woke from its waiting and climbed to me with a whirring that soothed me until I remembered Mr. Coughlan relied on the elevator when he was tired. I hadn't checked it or even cleaned it in days. It was a graceful antique, a workhorse. On its ceiling was a ring of old lights fit for a carnival, a merry-go-round. It had two doors. You could not see whether it was empty or not until you pulled open the first door with its gold-plated handle and small window, then the next, a slider that retreated automatically when the first door opened, and was fitted with the same window. My hands began trembling again. The hinges creaked, the aging sliding door serpentined slightly in its narrow tracks. No one there or not quite, for when I stepped inside, taking a full breath of what I thought would be relief, I took in an odor—ammonia first, the first note of what I recognized to be urine. It was so powerful, having been trapped, left to fester, that I stepped out and leaned back on the first thing I could. Mr. Coughlan's door, where his absence was now as alive, as unsettling, as the smell of piss in my elevator.

I used bleach. I did not care if it was remarked by the environmentally sensitive in the building. The discovery required something that matched, even overwhelmed it in its noxiousness. As I mopped out the elevator there was a suspension of noise, of everything, as if the building, out of respect, contained all its annoyances, all the nerves that were my tenants and their guests or the one guest. I thought of waking them, every single one—the vision of it gave life to my body—asking them without prefacing apologies when they'd seen Mr. Coughlan last. I wanted to draw them out of their dramas as surely as they'd wanted that of me on occasion, but I wouldn't. I would call his daughter directly, perhaps I would call the police myself—what was the etiquette? I did not know, but I knew the body's defections had to be addressed with efficiency and already I was behind. I still remembered my father cleaning up my vomit when I was a child, in the sore-making hours of the night or early morning; I remembered my mother's cool, thin hands on my hot face, steadying me through what she assured me was temporary. I held on to that sort of sweetness back when I contended with my husband's accidents, one after another. For him the messes his illness made were indignities and so it was up to me to wipe them away as quickly as they happened, as if they never had, this vigilance the only answer to the body's failures.

Back in my apartment, I peeled off my clothes and left them in a pile on the floor. I found Coughlan's daughter's number, dialed, but it was nearing 2 A.M. and I let it ring once before hanging up. I would try her and the police when it got light. I sat in my own favorite chair from which I watched the movies I liked, sometimes the news, listened to the radio, but it soon became Mr. Coughlan's chair and my body his, that heavy, that unknowable to me. I got up and paced until I couldn't and found myself in front of my medicine cabinet again. I had more than sleeping pills stored away on the shelves and under my sink, even in my fridge. There was morphine, in liquid, tablet, capsule, and sublingual forms: MSIR, MS Contin, Avinza, Oramorph, Roxanol. A whole language of opiates. Not to mention the liquid Ativan, tablets of Percocet, Xanax, Klonopin, Seconal. Most of the bottles bore my husband's name, a few my own. His doctor had been as forthcoming with his prescription pad as state and federal guidelines would allow. I'd intended to throw the stuff away many times but didn't. It wasn't just because of a pamphlet of Angie Braunstein's found under my door months and months ago, that had warned about the effect of discarded pharmaceuticals on the water supply; it spoke of fish with confused sexual physiognomy, of extra gills, depressed immune and nervous systems; fish drunk on Prozac, Ambien. The drugs had sustained my husband and me—the names and dates on the labels were there for me to see every time I reached for dental floss. Small markers. Memorials. Not a matter of choice for him then and often magical in their impact. Still potent for all these reasons even though the majority of the expiration dates had long since passed.

Our hospice nurse, Helen, believed in generous doses of palliatives for everyone, the terminal patient, the family of the terminal patient. She didn't believe pain had to be tolerated, or not forever. She'd send me to bed telling me I looked ratty, placing a pill square in my palm. "Grab on to it," she'd say. I had liked her—she was less reverent of death than the other nurses we auditioned. "You have some say in all this," she'd say, squeezing my arm. "So does he." She rarely spoke in a whisper or mooned at me sympathetically and always laughed with her mouth open— and I'd let myself fall asleep for short runs with her in the next room with him; I'd sometimes wake with the pill, having melted some, stuck to my hand. Now I swallowed a Xanax. I ran a bath.

I tried not to imagine where Mr. Coughlan could be or the variety of ways a city like this might harm him. I tried not to recall the smell in my elevator. The water ran too hot. I let it. I took a Seconal before I eased my way in.

The bell—my husband was meant to ring it when he needed me or the nurse. He used it to joke, ringing it when he knew I was on the toilet or phone, ringing it to show me this could all be a game until it wasn't and he rang for meds, to stop the pain. *Why don't we end this? Leave me with the bottle, baby. C'mon, this is nonsense. C'mon,* he'd urge, like we could shuffle this off, like, yes, of course, we had some say. At that stage he couldn't do it without me—he couldn't hold things in his own hands for long; sometimes he had difficulty swallowing and the coughing hurt. And so I told the noise—what I thought was him making his case again with the bell—*a little longer, I'm not ready.* But the sound kept at it until it became a bleat, then a buzz, teeth bared, cutting into my sleep just enough for me to feel the bed was damp, the ends of my hair too, and to see the light in the room was high and splashing, outlining a moving tree copse on the wall beside my bed, pressing the shadow of the windowpanes into the shade. Late-morning sunshine and what I knew now was the persistence of the outside door buzzer, someone wanting into my building, without delay.

I stood into a whirling; the room spun with me in it. I sat back down to stop it. I stood once more, reaching out to objects that seemed to shy and float from me. I made my way to the door, reassembling what I could of last night so that where I found myself now, as I pressed the front-door entrance release, could begin to feel real and firm, could matter again. The absence of sound, its teeth, slackened me, and when, at the sink, I brought cold water to my face, inside my mouth, my insides went cold and liquid, too. I put on my robe to warm myself, combed my hair away from my eyes, but everything lifted and sloshed as if in an Atlantic tide. *He loves the Maine coast and likes to tell me Long Island Sound is a sad dirty little pond.* Who was I telling? Helen. *Maybe we could bring him to Maine one more time.*

The bell rang again, but I noticed that now the sound was different, trilling, without that mad jangling. My own doorbell. Someone at *my* door. Pressing at my bell and then knocking. Alternating. Whoever it was didn't want to express politeness but that there was no time. I held on to the doorknob and felt the chill of its metal rush in waves into the current around me, pulling me away.

My mother can drive us up there so we can see to him, Helen. We can do it, for him. His last trip to the ocean.

If I could open the door, the thought occurred to me I could let the water out of the room, of me, but I risked letting something else in. Even so, I couldn't bear the cold—in me, in him—for much longer; his hands had become brittle icicles. And his coughing became choking— liquid where it should not have been. His body empty as a barrel, as rigid, too cold, yet flooding.

I made the decision, leaned into it, and before I'd fully opened the door, she was charging me—her face to mine already. Black hair moving, brown eyes flashing, as if with her wild pulse; her mouth open, wet and red inside with anger. "Why haven't you called? I'm sick, *sick* with worry!" Jeanie Coughlan stood as her father did—wide-stanced but in her case not to withstand outside weather but the weather inside her.

I struggled to find the thread that connected me to this—"I did call last night," I stammered, "but I hung up. It was late. I didn't realize how late. I intended to call first thing—"

"Did you? First thing? It's *nearly noon.*"

"I was up late. There was an incident or I mean something happened."

"To him?"

"No, no. It's nothing. Nothing. I'm sure he's fine. But the police. Have you called?"

"Do you even know when you last saw him?"

"Several days, maybe a week—" Dizzy, I was, remembering, trying to wake, his breathing so ragged.

She reared back. "*A week?!*"

"I cannot keep tabs on all my tenants—"

Her face aimed for mine, closer still. "But you can take their money, *his* money. *That* you would miss."

"Don't be silly. I care about your father."

"How dare you! You *care* about him and you let him come here? Where he's alone, where's there's no one to watch, to protect him. You don't bother to return my calls. Really, this is *too* much. I mean, who *are* you, anyway?"

I could not match her speed. "I'm not here to surveil your father. He came here because he didn't want that. He's capable—"

"*Capable?* How would you know? What do you know about him—"

"I know he loves his freedom, his privacy—"

She spoke over me: "Who are you but the woman who takes his money? Who has no care for his family's wishes? A parasite, that's what you are, a goddamned—"

We shouldn't live like this, Celia. C'mon, honey.

Her mouth became a bell, jangling—alarm, alarm.

C'mon, this has gone on too long.

I could not conceive of killing my husband, but I could arrange a last ocean view. Jeanie could not keep her father safe or make him heed her, but she could scold me, turn me villain, make me share the awful pressure of her fear. Our half measures, our bait-and-switches in the face of suffering which are themselves a sorrow, a provocation.

Her mouth could not stop. It spit and sprayed my face as she tried to climb inside me and turn me interior side out, to locate the size and range of my culpability.

I broke in, "I'm sure he'll be fine. I'm sure he *is* fine."

I was not certain she heard me even as I tightened my jaw, gritted my teeth, endeavored to form a smile that would reassure as I had done for my husband. *More time, darling, we need more time,* my jaw aching, counting his breaths . . . I interjected again, with determined lightness, "You two will laugh—" but before I could finish, I saw Mr. Coughlan's daughter's hand shoot up from her side; I saw an instant of white palm and then took the hot flat of it to my face. My jaw rattled open, my neck twisted as my head, loose and wet, bounced to the side. She'd hit me hard and knocked the water out of me and the sting she left on my cheek spread like wildfire through my face into my body. I was finally awake and perceived just how close she was to me as she strained to dive inside me; I saw the pattern of pores in her skin, stray blood vessels, and freckles on her nose, which had amassed to form a shadow of pigment; I saw scarlet fissures in her eyes, clotting them; and that she would keep coming, that she couldn't help herself. I found my balance, checked the solidity of the wood under my feet, and struck her in the same manner as she had me, as hard and as completely. My whole arm tingled; my hand smarted; it had found bone under the softness of her cheek. *No, no, we shouldn't live like this.*

She stepped back then, and then again, covering the spot where I'd hit her with both her hands, as if to preserve the sensation. She had been shocked elsewhere, forcibly brought here, just as I had been. She was calm when she said, "I'm going to call the police."

"I think you should," I told her, swallowing, pretending poise, even as I was on fire. I nodded at her, but not just her, because when she retreated from me I could finally take in the fullness of the hall. We were not alone. Hope stood at the top of the flight of stairs there, a hand on the banister, watching and seeing all there was to see.

LADY INTO FOX

———

I WAS, OR HAD BECOME, a woman who if hit, hit back. And a woman? I'd hit a woman. I let this dawn on me not once but as many times as it took to address what assailed me next—remorse, pleasure, fear. More fear.

The adrenaline. The sudden strength in my arm, and then the terror of it. My own unpredictability, something I thought I'd mastered in these years here, in my building. I'd chosen my tenants with care. I'd kept to myself. These choices had contained me, but now? I was failing somehow. We were not safe.

The next day, once all my tenants were gone, I didn't hesitate: I gathered all the keys to the apartments (keys, after all, that were mine as much as theirs). I had little choice. That delicious and horrible adrenaline a threat. I couldn't sit still now. Yes, I'd wanted certain barriers, believed in privacy, the right to it, but as landlady I decided who had earned that right from me. Certainly I did not think Mr. Coughlan's disappearance directly related to my other tenants, but the tenor of the building had changed so much lately, and I needed to take the care I had failed to in the last few weeks. I had to see everything there was to see. Get clear. Some things we are helpless before; other circumstances require agency: acting before we are too alone with our choices, or lack of them. Mr. Coughlan had stepped out of the building as if stepping off a cliff and no one had been alert enough to remark it or stop it.

I knocked before I unlocked the Braunstein door. I gave a hello as I moved into the living room and was confronted not just by how entirely these rooms had been claimed from me but with what confidence. Furniture had been shoved into the middle of the room. Lamps without lampshades had been posted around to better light the walls. Each of these was freshly painted again; each room yet a new and emphatic color—the orangest orange, a cerulean blue, a brick red; this time, she'd not spared the moldings I had stripped and sanded to wood years ago. Angie was experimenting and didn't see the use in asking permission now, four years in. She'd supplied herself with what the cans told me was the sort of paint that wouldn't harm fish or fowl and gave the rooms a peppery new-car smell; she'd taken down her Amnesty International map of the world that I'd noticed on my last visit when a hissing radiator valve needed replacing. She'd removed her tribal masks from what she once told me was Papua New Guinea and placed them on her coffee table face up in a neat row as if to make sure they were comfortable, had enough air ("You never hear about the AIDS epidemic in PNG because its geography isn't relevant to U.S. interests, but it's like *totally* out of control").

In a cursory glance at the kitchen I saw dishes piled in the sink, herbs drying on the windowsill, and at least four or five instances of "non-toxic" or "organic" advertised in bold and in bolder colors on labels—on dishwashing soap, rice protein powder, bread, and apples as big as a man's fist. On the table was a box full of handouts, how-to's, how not-to's, sign-up sheets, ragged pens, along with an ancient-looking steno pad. I scanned it to find a catalog of statistics on infant mortality rates, CO_2 emissions, and clitorectomies as well as names, even mine, alongside of which she recorded the info she had shared. Mr. Coughlan's name was not there, as if he didn't exist anymore or perhaps never had, but Hope's was, already; beside it Angie wrote in red ink with exclamations, "recycling procedures—update building."

The bedroom appeared intact or to my eyes it was. The room had eastern and southern light, a constant companionable light, or that's how I viewed it when I prepared the space for occupants years ago.

George's and my bedrooms fell in the same line as theirs,

but trees and adjacent buildings kept us from having the same share of the day. I had hoped a room rarely cast in shadow would make life's complications more tolerable, less monolith.

On the dresser sat a framed photo of Mitchell standing with natives from a place from which I imagined celebrities stole children these days. There were two shirtless boys showing ribs with Mitchell between them. They all smiled but squinted and looked uncomfortable. Still they did what they were told—the husband in particular, on a trip arranged by his wife, did what he was told.

Their bed, smothered in down comforter dressed in a light pink duvet, was only a double, though there was plenty of room for a queen or a king. Over the bed hung a tapestry. I took it to be contemporary Indian or a good imitation of it and something that maybe Mitchell had insisted on. The colors were calmer and simpler than any other in the apartment—a moon the color of rosy flesh bled in small streams into an expanse of blue.

I searched for more of Mitchell in the closet—a walk-in. I'd provided two bars for hanging shirts and pants and a higher bar for women's dresses, long coats. Mitchell had been apportioned less than half of the space yet his belongings were sturdier, stiffer, and more uniform. They had the authority of men's clothes—fewer required to be well-dressed, suit jackets designed to suggest strength and symmetry in the shoulders. I put my nose to the tweed, the wool sweaters, the synthetic of his parka, his windbreaker. I still had some of my husband's clothes, but I had put them out of reach, where I could not keep touching them and looking in his pockets for clues to days he could not have back. My hands now dug in Mitchell's jacket pockets—they found change, a fortune-cookie fortune, an ATM receipt, a matchbook. All the comforting debris of a gender not given to carrying compacts or combs, those bits of reassurance to one's appearance.

Because I could not resist, I ran a seam of a pair of rayon dress pants between my fingers; at the pocket I heard a crunch of paper. I pulled out a note composed in a hand I didn't know; it read, "I'll wait for you." I judged it a woman's writing because of the way the letters swooped and danced yet were modest, not wide, minding the space they took up, but then I was no expert and couldn't remember what Mitchell's handwriting looked like. "I'll wait for you" could mean nothing—I'll wait for you at the dry cleaner's or the dentist's or after work—or it could mean everything—authored by the woman on the Promenade, who was as slight as Mitchell, perhaps as crowded by her choices. When I reached to return the note to the pants, I dropped it. It fell as open as a hand. I thought to leave it there. Instead, I picked it up, folded it in half, then quarters, and slid it into my own pocket.

Hope had left George's door unlocked and the flowers she'd collected, days—even weeks—old now, to dry in their vases. I called out to her and felt how foolish it was to speak a name like hers out loud, to no one in particular.

I nearly tripped over a cord connected to a vacuum cleaner. Though it was plugged in, it had been abandoned before it could do its job, judging from the petals and other detritus on the floor. A bottle of Pledge and a rag had also been made ready. Evidently she'd intended to tackle the place and the soft moss she'd thrown over it—tried to imagine something more orderly—but gave up before she began.

I was glad to see George's lamp was unhurt.

In the kitchen wine bottles drained of wine—red and white—had been put in a paper bag, dishes soaked in soapy water, and the gardenia now sat on George's cherry table. Its blossoms were gone (of their own accord or Hope's I couldn't say), but its leaves were still shining, making of their deep green a sort of decadence. There was a bruise on the wall where it had met the table over and over, but I told myself it was barely there and fixable besides. In place of that noise and motion—a scene I could still see in my mind's eye—there was now this otherworldly plant, a well-intentioned gift from a daughter to her mother, that in doing nothing was doing everything—taking the light in the silence of an empty apartment.

George's orchids, three of them, every one temperamental, were arranged like carolers around the bedroom window closest to the bed. While they were not in full flower, buds dotted the stems and their pot soil was damp, attended to. Outside all the windows, the trees tossed—how quickly they'd come to us this spring and with what extravagance, and the room, its blinds open, now tilted with them, the sun and trees in competition for stretches of the room, turning shadows into liquid and the furniture into shapeshifters. Perhaps that's why Hope had not made the bed with any real care—she'd been in a hurry to get into the day and thrown the covers up and over the pillows, but on one side they dragged and lumped on the floor. I watched her go that morning with her hands carting crisp-looking shopping bags; whether she was returning items or giving gifts I couldn't say, though I anticipated it would take time, at least a ride to Manhattan and back. When I heard her rustle down the stairs and out the door earlier, I'd stepped out of sight. I did not want to invite any more commentary about yesterday's incident.

Yes, yes, as soon as Mr. Coughlan's daughter marched off to call the police, and Hope and I were alone, Hope had given me a crackling smile from the top of the stairs. Her eyebrows lifted, her aspect gaining in glee, she looked about to laugh or clap her hands or both. Before she could, I said, "I'm sorry you had to see that." I said this as solemnly as I could given how my insides jumped.

"I'm not!" she called—her delight charging my door as I swung it shut.

In the bedroom now, smelling her rose and rosemary scent, the stubborn savory and sweet of her, the room content to be in league with the new trees, I resisted straightening the bed, but once my hand touched the cool of the bedspread's cotton, it gripped and tugged in favor of a little symmetry, just enough not to be noticed. When I moved closer to make a few adjustments, I kicked something—an open notebook that had been concealed under the bedcover—a pretty leather-bound thing with the outline of a tear-shaped leaf stamped into its front. On the visible pages was a long list, banal enough at first.

Dentist appointment
Lawyer's fee
Buy Danielle boots, Bendel's
My garden

Her handwriting varied from neat to loose—ends of words became lines, longish dashes, best guesses as to what they spelled out. I puzzled it through.

Metrocard/subway
Gynecologist
A good stew with sirloin? Clark Street butcher. Grass-fed.
Black-eyed peas?
HIS favorite
Gray hairs on his earlobes. Two hard gray hairs on one lobe,
    three on the other. How long have they been there now?
Five years? Six.
Not a young man anymore. He can't bear it.

She left the rest of that page blank. The next began with

K-Y
Call D's lawyer
Leo and gallery opening
Bendel's?
J's birthday
Mole by his heart. It started to feel like a scab under my
　　finger. The appointment I made with the dermatolo-
　　gist. Did he remember to go?
And the blue suit. The suit he'd walked home to us in.
　　Will he ever wear it again? . . . No.
How to shake him <u>out, out, out?</u>
Les.

I turned the pages, went backward and found more lists of chores and reminders and then interruptions of prose, sometimes long, sometimes short, not always entirely legible—I couldn't be sure of what I read.

That vein on your calf, climbing up the inside of your leg. Every year it is darker and thicker and you rub it like it's a rash. You and our children and every room we've lived in under my skin. . . .

Lester. A man outrunning his name. Has he? Yes. . . . Money and adventure for him. He tells me I can be any woman I want to be. I cannot open my legs for long before he hits against old habits and you with me everywhere inside me and everywhere I go. Your preferences, 25 years of what makes you laugh, what pleases you. You walking home to me in a blue suit covered in dust, when so many husbands did not . . .

A page later after a reminiscence about a meal had in Rome where the truffle oil was like "heaven poured into me":

To be made ashamed of years lived, of the commitments we've made. We have our experience but are not to show it. It can't live on the face or sink the breasts. If it does, it's our fault. Our shame. To age means we are not doing things right, not loving ourselves as we are asked to love others, everyone, our children, our friends, his friends, his family, their children, taking them in, all their problems, their empty stomachs, their dirty laundry. Danny scrutinizes my skin, my hair, as if an answer is there. Les slapped me across the face. I did not feel it or not as pain. He fucks a dead woman.

Isolated on its own page, left in the middle of it:

He says he loves her. I fell in love. I fell in love, he says. After all these years. How could this happen? Love her out of my sight, I told him.

And from an entry I took to be more recent:

Les has bought me clothes. The silliest stuff. Porn fantasia
*   extraordinaire. I will return them. . . .*
I must tell D to wear her hair down more often. All I see
*   is her father's ears.*
Script for sleep.
Lawyer
Neosporin

I closed the book, held it to me. My heart beat against
it. I opened it again to look for my name. I then pieced together the details of a spaghetti squash recipe, just as she
had, out of order. A half hour in the oven at 350. And I
found a list for George's party, of food and people. My
name was there and "stern creature??" and after it, "sad."

I scolded myself and put the book in the approximate
position in which I found it, partially covered by the bed
linens. When I pushed it perhaps a shade too far, its corner made an object roll, a glass from the sound of it—a
wineglass in fact, on its side. A trail of dried red led out of
the glass. I got on hands and knees to locate the stain, the
extent of it. I made out one great drop the size of an Indian dollar deep as blood in George's tan Kashan rug. I put
my finger on it, could feel a trace of stickiness. I could get
it out, if I was permitted. I carried the glass to the kitchen
and slid it into the soapy water. I looked for it to settle,
listened for it. Waited.

I did not want to go—I half-willed her to walk in and discover me in the apartment—mine by rights and more so in George's absence. Maybe I'd say I smelled gas or maybe I'd stand there in the middle of her tide and let her see it as I did, rising and rising unmindful of charts or the lives of others.

Back in my apartment an unfamiliar male voice greeted me. I went for my golf club, one of my father's old drivers, until I put together that my voice mail, provided by the phone company, must have been full so the call had gone to my phone's old answering system and was recording, out loud. The voice's cadence and inflection was Bay Ridge or Staten Island and glad to be aligned there; it never-minded g's at the end of words and rolled through consonants like they were buttery things in its mouth.

It was a police officer. He was calling to "ask some questions about a Mr. Joseph Coughlan, to confirm specifics given to me by Jeanette Coughlan, about her father's disappearance." He spoke quickly so by the time I ran to the phone and picked up the receiver, the voice was gone, already on to the next call, the next set of inquiries. A checklist. Pro forma.

I gripped the hard of the phone's plastic in my hand and went blank, listening to the dial tone. There in that drift I saw myself call my husband's sister, to tell her things that I had not. Did she know my husband had believed we would live in Umbria's Valnerina or on Lake Como, maybe do a stint in Turkey or Greece one day? Where we'd raise children who spoke in English fizzy with foreign words? Or when we walked over the Brooklyn Bridge that he'd touch the Brooklyn-side stanchion, every time, to thank the bridge, reassure it?

She certainly couldn't know that the last book I read to him when he was still healthy enough to follow it was *Lady into Fox,* a slim fantastic story about a woman who transforms into a fox during a walk in the woods with her husband. Not a masterpiece but unexpected and sweetly mournful, so delightful to us both. I had the very copy, bought secondhand—it still smelled of the white bean soup he'd always make, that I prepared for him that day. I'd trapped it all, the book, its garlic aroma, in a Ziploc. And did she know how many times he'd asked me to restore him, healthy again, in my head and heart, giving not a cell, an inch, nothing to the wasting man who had, as he put it, only one good trick in him? No, she didn't know.

Neither did my mother.

What I wouldn't give to hear her voice just then. She'd be walking the beach or dancing or preparing to do one or the other. Heat coming off her skin.

She drank for a time after my father died in his golf club's bar seven years ago. He had loved golf and the one drink that he allotted himself after his eighteen holes—a Manhattan or a vodka martini depending on the season. He died of an aneurism before he finished it so my mother finished it for him over and over, for about ten months, with dedication, until without much planning she decided to fly to Florida to see a high school friend. She went dancing at a supper club early into the visit, went again. She stopped drinking the next day, and when her impulses quarreled with her she walked the beach until her legs hurt. A long weekend's trip turned into a month's stay and a condo rental. Within two weeks she met a man who liked to dance. Within a year she sold our house in Connecticut and moved to Venice Beach. Now she danced up and down the Florida coast, the Gulf side. She had shoes with silver bows and dresses with rhinestones in them. She could drink the occasional glass of champagne, took courage from the *Oprah* show, and was still beautiful. She hoped I would move down there one day; she sent real estate listings. Even though I'd visited only briefly, after my husband's death, and not again in almost two years, she was undaunted. Once, after she'd learned I'd bought my building, she said, "He's not coming back," another time that Brooklyn was stale now, soured—didn't I feel it? Where were my eyes? My nose? My heart? Why was I so rigid and, she said without saying so, unlike her?

A stern creature, she wouldn't argue, no, but my husband loved New York City, and I had made promises to him, to all his live affections. He even loved its subway when I did not, had not, even just to ride and watch, to be mesmerized bodily by its motion. . . . He knew the city's history better than most—he'd grown up in two of the five boroughs till he was eleven and from the Detroit suburbs, where his family moved, read about New York like other boys read about Tolkien's Middle Earth. It was his mythical place; he thought nothing more soothing or thrilling than the sound of the Staten Island Ferry's blowing horns heard throughout the Heights every half hour. Perhaps that is why I could never refuse Mr. Coughlan—my ferryman. I replaced the receiver. The dial tone had become a warning.

I still could find little impulse in me to justify to anyone the choices that shaped my days since I was widowed, matching them against convention. Lately, increasingly, events risked overwhelming any choice anyway, as if currents I could not see had been made to race. Hurry. Hurry. I took my coat. I'd find him or so I reassured myself. It was not impossible anyway.

NO LOITERING

———

OUTSIDE, THE WIND STILL ROILED the new green leaves. They filled out the world of the Brooklyn streets, making you forget all the spaces that only a short time ago were wide open with desolation, the sort particular to winter in the city: variations of gray, the hard outlines of branches, wires, concrete. Yes, all those open mouths saying nothing and everything for so long were filled to the brim, hidden, and so beside the point now. Faces on the street tried to register this, how everything had softened and with it, the faces, too, trying to keep up, with the new season and its requirements.

I looked for Mr. Coughlan on benches, under them. I scanned the streets so refigured. I passed through Clinton

Park and went north, into the Heights, to do a turn in Cadman Plaza Park. They'd put in a new jogging path made of what felt like cork underfoot.

I forced myself to look into the diners on Montague. The bars weren't open yet, but the pear trees up and down the street were still startling, as if someone had snapped a switch a week or so ago and shocked them all white, alive, otherworldly, and the magnolia so heavy with blossoms on the corner of Clinton had already dropped a few petals. The wind could not help but disturb it.

I did not go down into the subway easily. Twice I started down and came back up. One last time, I stopped to breathe, waited to feel the wind stir my hair and the debris on the stairs to the R train. One stop to Whitehall—the Staten Island Ferry stop. I'd not ridden the subway in some time and only when I had no other option.

What seemed another life, what was in fact, when I was married to a healthy young man and I worked an office job full-time, I took the subway every day. I rushed in, through the turnstile, into the elevator, its surfaces doused with ammonia, clock ticking in my heart, numbers—of time, money—full of significance to me then ticking too, adding up and up, so high where I had a vision of the future. Things I wanted to come true set up on stilts. I exited the elevator with other bodies, racing them down more stairs, hating the other commuters, as they did me, hating the train for not arriving as I did. On the platform,

I always stared at a block of dark, from which the train would emerge, making bargains with it if it would come now, no, *now,* now. I avoided the dripping water deforming the tile and cement below, where it had landed over time, a long time it had been dripping. Already, the chalky captive air was in my nose, and I found myself watching the tails of the rats on the empty tracks waving at me, serpentining. I did not want to make a study of them or the endless patterns of ancient peeling paint overhead. The city never seemed to have enough resources to show these stations any love, not even in tony Brooklyn Heights. Now most of the city's resources went to security. Men in uniform, whether NYPD or National Guard, with guns, sometimes dogs. More necessity. Another form of ugly. Alerts issued. Alerts distrusted.

It used to make me laugh to watch the visiting Europeans; they were less fearful; as if New York was a European outpost and, when the dollar declined, a playground, a mall. In English, in French, Spanish, languages I'd studied, they dared to call the city beautiful. Yes, Fifth Avenue, the skyline, the Bridge, Central Park, what was left of the Plaza, the consuming energy, the efficiency of commerce even after 9/11. But I always wanted to correct them. Explain that they did not see what we saw every day—before and after the towers fell—or smell what we did and wear that smell on their clothes, in their hair. If there was beauty for its everyday citizens, it hid and threaded through the ugliness.

Some mornings, back then, not all, it depended, I saw it from where I stood on the subway platform. However many of us there were bent toward the tunnel, watching that same dense, dusty dark. So many mornings spent attending the dark there, praying to it, and just as impatience grew into shifting and sighing and swearing, there'd be an intimation of light on the tunnel wall. The darkness would jump and give way in a flash then return, only to be pierced by a sliver that became a fine line, all made from light and as delicate as anything was delicate. The light grew, in squares and streaks, agitating faster and faster, spreading in the way only light or joy can spread, catching and unpredictable, and unless you were insensate your body woke with it and vibrated with the metal and hot air and noise—such affronting noise!—that was the arriving train. You'd be exhilarated, or I was. All sorts of human traffic—need and boredom and anger—awaited you on that train, but for a moment, ears ringing, you ran in, delirious for motion.

Today, rush hour over, the platform felt a vacuum, very little of the spring day could be felt, save perhaps in the clothing and attitude of a few stragglers, in no hurry at this hour. The train could soon be heard rumbling its way to us before it was visible. I'd forgotten that was sometimes so, here at the Court Street stop, when the system had calmed. Then the train pulled in, making its outsized racket, a hundred strongmen banging on steel, metal brakes turning banshees, piercing the soft parts of you. I leaned into its wind, as close to the tracks as I could. When the doors opened, I hesitated only an instant, catching my breath.

Everything inside reflected, the ads for vodka and podiatric care, all the hard surfaces. The car was perhaps a third full. I sat diagonal to a young woman who dashed blush on her cheeks. It went on micaed and tropical. She held up a mirror, peered at herself with terrible seriousness. Lipstick came next. Another version of pink, of summer, of freshness. She did not seem to care who watched. I did in flashes. A Hassidic man, a seat over from me, with a dark beard, dark eyes, coat and hat, stared steadily. Not once did she give him the satisfaction of a look in reply.

Elsewhere on the car, fingers twitched on gadgets, a few heads were plugged up with white earphones. At one end of the car, a lanky boy drew an electronic game to his nose; its screen lit his eyes and blued his forehead. His long thumbs never stopped; they beat and poked and jabbed, faster and faster, as if the train's speed and not just the game he played dictated.

So much potential energy expressed in the congress of person and device, designed to claim the entitlements of privacy in public, to avert the eyes and more. One man held up a *Daily News*. No books today. I used to keep track of what was being read: Dean Koontz, Patricia Cornwell, Nelson DeMille, Stephen King. I'd seen Woolf, too, Virginia, and Chekhov and Calvino, but admittedly not as often, and then there were so many books I was not equipped to categorize, many in other languages, alphabets. I worked in book publishing back then, for a small literary house, and I believed with a young person's conviction that certain books, the right books, were a measure of a person's ambition to engage with life rather than retreat from it. If I saw a book held up that I admired, I'd look to see if my face or one I'd recognize was there behind it. More often than not, I'd get warning looks. There was never enough distance down here, so we were meant not to be too curious, not to wonder at one another too long.

The man a seat over from me now leaned into the aisle that separated him from the girl. He wanted her to see him. She still refused. She dug a nail around the outline of her lips to ensure her bright lipstick was not bleeding. Still he leaned, and my neck grew hot, itchy. I was a woman who hit back, or was I really? That anxiety. New unknowns and especially so here, on these live machines, where I'd given myself away before.

Five years ago, more, it had begun. Yes, my first long day as a widow. On that day, I had not held up a newspaper or hung over a book. I had death in my mouth, hands, hair, all over my skin. I had let go of all protections. I had looked at the man looking at me, for me. My clothes were thin, I was thin and thinning still, all of me untended to. I had goose bumps from the air-conditioning set for a July day in New York. Yes, the man whose cheeks looked freshly slapped had shifted his seat at least four times until he was next to me and breathing in my ear. He said, "I got fired today." He had something Eastern European in his accent and in the wide set of his brows and straw-colored hair sticky with gel. When I did not look at him or say anything in reply, but nodded slightly and kept my eyes straight ahead, he went further: "I would like to get with you." He smelled of Ivory soap and a persistent, vinegary sweat. "I think you would like that, too." I still did not look at him, only nodded again, glad to be taken from the horrible repetition of my thoughts.

I maintained my silence and kept my eyes from him as best I could throughout the episode. This made him bolder, though he had to work up to it through four station stops. Find the language that fit, the right level of force with me. I nearly laughed when he called me "bitch" the first time; not only was it a word from another world, it had a querying tone, as if he wanted me to approve it. When I would not kiss him at first, he pulled my hair but not hard, not right away. He had led me to the men's room of a deserted diner. Me, a nursemaid, a bookish woman, and that day, a new widow to someone I'd loved more than I did myself.

To the man half-asleep behind the register, he asked for a key and handed the man a limp bill. It may have only been a dollar. Once he latched the door, he positioned me against the sink, yanked down my drawstring pants, and then his voice went soft and stuttery as he explained that I was nobody now and that he owned me, that this was what

I always wanted and needed as a woman, that we would do this as many times and in as many ways as he needed because he was "my boss now." His phrase. Almost gentle like a young doctor instructing his patient if not for the violent bright of the fluorescent showing the grime everywhere and the sneer that kept steeling his mouth. I moved how and where he asked and when he could not come as he took me from behind he started hitting me on my back, first with an open hand and then a fist. He asked me to say things. I wouldn't at first. Pleasing him was not the point. He knocked my head against the mirror. Then I did.

He was after predictable things. But the words, as over-circulated as they are, can and do alter wildly with the scenario; they are porous so become filled with the squeaking timbre of the man's voice, with the hollowness of your own; there's the banality of the broken soap dispenser as you say *fuck me,* the haze and brown age spots of an ancient mirror over the sink as you say *that feels good,* and the blessed strangeness of it, degradation I'd allowed that day. I was wet, actually for a time, out of gratitude perhaps, that this act was nothing I would mourn as I was mourning suddenly and would yet mourn. That was the point, that day and on others to come. I had bruises, abrasions inside me, on my forehead, backside for weeks after, but, like Hope, I had hardly felt them either.

———

I missed my stop. I'd been pulled under. I became another vibrating body thrown in on itself, remembering to the rhythm of the train, of other bodies, half there, coming and going, seeing and not seeing. The girl and her makeup were gone. As was her admirer.

At Union Square, I turned around, went back south. It exhausted me, the effort, made me feel too acutely that so much of human life is deciding when to resist and when not to, when you can be carried and when you cannot, cannot afford to be.

Because I was weary as I reached the ferry terminal, where I came to search for Mr. Coughlan, the effects of the place did not dawn on me right away. The high ceilings, glass walls, its white metal bones. Its own environment much like an airport. What I did see as I climbed the escalator to the main concourse was a handful of security guards, chatting in desultory poses, half-bored. The patches on their blue jackets indicated they belonged to a private company. A few held yellow Labs on loose leashes. Affable, smiling dogs, tongues hanging. You had to pass through a line of low-grade metal detectors the size of tombstones to get to the waiting area. No one remarked me as I passed. There were only three shops: a bakery, a newspaper stand, and a deli; and lines of benches were made of a brindled brown and gray granite that sent a chill through me when I sat down.

Another security guard stood in the far corner of the structure, on the side with the Statue of Liberty to his left, behind him. The harbor's green lady was too far away and too small at this distance to be sure of what she was holding up (though I knew what it was; didn't we all?), but from that distance it was clear only that she did so without fail, whatever the weather. I raised myself up and walked over to the man. I was too worn to smile convincingly so I didn't. The water just outside took the sun and threw it in my eyes.

"I'm looking for a friend, a tenant of mine," I told the man carefully, squinting. "He was a ferryman in his day. I thought maybe he'd visit here, want to ride the ferry. He's an older man, white-haired, not tall." The face I addressed myself to was impassive with wide planes; bags tried to hide his eyes and his lips were dry.

"Lady, a lot of people pass through here—"

"Of course, I thought maybe he'd ride back and forth or maybe he'd sit here, for the view." He looked over his shoulder briefly to check the view, as if to verify we saw the same thing.

"No one's allowed to stay on the boat anymore. They have to get off if they want to get on again, and we don't encourage multiple trips." He had no yellow Lab of his own, this man. He crossed his arms. I guessed he wasn't far from retirement. His skin was the color of teak yet still managed to be sallow. "They get on here," he pointed to loading doors 1 and 2, "get off there," then to a corridor that separated the disembarking from the waiting area. Traffic control.

"I'll wait and see. Thank you."

He said nothing in reply, only looked me up and down, not with derision, but because suspicion was part of the job, of the urban days we shared now. It was also a punctuation mark: He returned to surveilling the great hall, had other things, people, to watch.

Back in my stone seat, all I saw was outside, how the breeze ran over the water's surface, stirring the sunlight there, turning it into waves. New Jersey's shore across the way, to the west, was hazy with green growth and made to seem paltry, a scattered strip under the dominance of sky.

The security man stalked off to join his coworkers; I heard a shot of laughter. Maybe they were tickled by the woman who thought they would recognize one old man in thousands of travelers, or by the notion that all old ferrymen collected here. Or maybe not, maybe I did not matter much. It was far-fetched that I'd find him—I knew that as well as they did—but I liked all the sky offered here. So would Mr. Coughlan. Of that I was certain, and it consoled me. It was not always easy to know expanse, real expanse in New York City, unless you were determined or rich. Most of us here traded in confines—of a train, an office, an apartment under or over a stack of them, of streets lined with tall structures that divvy up and often block the light. But here expanse, along with the day's generosity or lack of it, depending on the weather and season, was given on all sides of the high glass box. Trees from Battery Park at the right edge of the view shook their moving parts in the air.

I closed my eyes, memorizing it all, imagining room inside me for all of it, leaves shaking, clouds splitting, blue as vast backdrop to this and me and more, and feeling something loosen ever so slightly. It was worth the visit, to see what I could see. I considered riding to the other side, but I'd last ridden the ferry with my husband, from the old terminal. How he'd liked to stand in the front of the boat on the lower deck and whoop and laugh at the motion. He was, at times, vengeful in his pursuit of joy, of new air. It exhilarated me, his boldness; it made me bold. I hollered too, at the air, the screaming birds, at ghosts, as he'd like to describe them to me—of the British, who'd seized Staten Island at the start of the Revolutionary War, the same forces who soon occupied Manhattan and made its occupants suffer at every opportunity and those occupants who endured it rather than see their city burn. Ah, but those Staten Islanders (*right there!*), they wanted to secede from New York City as recently as 1989; they were still part of a place apart, their own island.

We did not have to get off then to come back, so we did not—we were allowed to be children at sea, so we were—but now passengers were required to get off. If Mr. Coughlan was on the incoming ferry, he would have to pass by me if he meant to keep crossing the harbor.

Around me a press of bodies would eventually form. A

woman yanked her small son to his feet to walk until, exasperated by his refusal, she lifted him off the ground by his arm. A girl yelled at what I took to be her boyfriend, "Why you gotta say those things to me?"

"Can't I be me? Be who I *really* am?" he replied.

Then they were gone, the smells of sweat and food and perfume, the conflicts, pleasure bolting to hit the high ceiling, the leisurely postures, shreds of conversations, of sex, and we few were left alone again. I was glad each time and also sad, inexplicably, for a moment, not to get up and go with the rest. Perhaps from some strange or ancient part of me missing the comforts of the pack.

I tried to sort through the exiting passengers, filing through the corridor now. If he was among them, yes, as unlikely as that was, I knew I would spot him, even if I did not stand and press my face to the glass. He had a very particular carriage; he still had power in his arms and shoulders and they pumped with greater strength than the rest of him moving him along. He'd be wearing a cap, his ancient weather-resistant parka.

I had the sense that someone was looking at me; I turned to see the security guard from the corner approaching. Maybe he planned to ask me to move on. No loitering, or not for long, since 9/11. He had a slight catch in his gait, a vulnerability in the knee, or perhaps the hip. A short-waisted man, his legs were long and thin; he operated them as if he was made to think about the bones inside them too keenly. I ducked my head. Whatever it was about sitting here and letting the fullness of the space work on me made me quick to emotion. For a second, I thought I might cry if he asked me to leave. "Ma'am," he said in greeting, though he was older than me by at least twenty years. He eased himself onto the bench a few spots down from me. He leaned in, a confiding posture, his face more mobile than before, better circulated. Something in him had shifted as he watched me waiting for one old man or maybe it was the laughter he'd shared with his coworkers. How funny that is, under the right mix of circumstances, how we move in and out of our default attitudes, how we open and close.

"Ma'am, one of the guys thinks he saw your man. An old captain, right?"

I nodded.

"He went over and back. Got off, got back on. Three or four times, they say. He talked up the guys, they let him shadow the deckhands. But that was a week or more ago. There's been no sign of him since."

"But he was all right?"

"Seemed to them he was."

"To who?"

"Frank," he said, pointing. Frank waved. "And Bobby, a deckman."

"Is Bobby here?"

"Not today. He's off today but usually he's on one of the boats."

"Can I speak to Frank?"

"I don't see why not."

"He's my tenant, Mr. Coughlan, my tenant. He's not come home in many days now. His daughter is worried. The police have been called."

"His home is that." He pointed to the water. "Or that's my guess. Those old captains?" He smiled at something unseen. "They got balls."

I walked back home this time—I didn't need the subway anymore; I walked over the Brooklyn Bridge. You were made to climb the bridge, up to its high suspension over the river, the cables gleaming just as they were designed to, and because as you walked, climbing, you could not yet see the bridge's midpoint, its other side, you could fool yourself into believing you were traveling into something unforeseen. The tourists and strangers climbed with and around you; people covered their faces with their cameras or aimed their one-eyed cell phones at the view. Windbreakers and khakis, western travel gear. All of us with either nothing in common or so much, depending on your vantage, at least sharing a direction, to climb and cross.

When a girl approached me to take a photo—*would you? please, thank you*—I didn't consider refusing her. A university-age girl from somewhere Scandinavian, from the looks of it, traveling with her mother and younger sister through New York's cold spring; all three made me think of oversized daisies and of the boons of being foreign and blond, of living out of reach of or at least some distance from urban American habits and our overweening American expectations.

The currents of air switched and tossed their yellow hair—they laughed at this and couldn't stop laughing; their laughter so much the same. I had to move them against the stanchion my husband had often touched as we passed, out of the way of the wind and the foot and bike traffic, so I could capture all three faces without obstruction or eyes squeezed shut with hilarity. I laughed too and still had Frank's voice in my ears instructing me just before I had moved on that Mr. Coughlan was "a tough old guy." The sentiment relaxed me, so I did not mind the small talk on the bridge. *We are on holiday. We've left the men at home.* Brothers or boyfriends or a father. I didn't know exactly and it didn't matter. *New York we find so very loud and pretty,* and I agreed because it was right then, with the water ruffling below us, tugs muscling through the harbor, the old bridge seeming so resolute underfoot. *I hope you have a lovely visit,* I told them, and as the women gave me more pleases and thank-yous, I heard Frank the security guard assure me, "He's no fool and sometimes we all want to walk out, you know? Vanish. Like that." All his peers standing with us had assured me, just as the first guard had done, that ferry captains needed more freedom than most of us. I chose to believe them and now smiled through my goodbyes and the girl handing me her e-mail on a blue scrap of paper. *If you're ever in Aarhus, let me know. We will show you around. Come in the spring! Oh, of course,* I said, as if that was as likely as anything else. Denmark in the spring.

CONSENTING ADULTS

___

As SOON AS I was on land again, cutting home through
Cadman Plaza Park, I felt my stomach go into crisis. I had
forgotten to eat. I bought a roast chicken, cooked just that
afternoon and warmed under lights; a hunk of hard Gruyère;
celery and carrots; hummus; freshly baked, soft-in-the-
middle chocolate-chip cookies; and a slice of blueberry pie.
I had those Danish girls in mind when I detoured for a
bottle of Argentinian Malbec. I imagined I'd somehow invite the girls to my building, lead them into my garden
with wineglasses overflowing, and tell what I planned on
planting, daisies, hydrangeas, and Bermuda freesia, even if
freesia would not survive here. Yes, I felt magnanimous,
and when I made it home and laid my groceries out on the

table, I ripped a leg off the chicken and ate it as if I were an amiable giant with an amiable giant's appetite. The warm oil of the dark meat slipped down my throat and gave me more license, breaking open a current of thrilling prerogatives. Yes, men like Mr. Coughlan need more air. Denmark in May or early June. How long had it been since I'd traveled or taken a photo? I drank the Malbec from the bottle. Though I tried not to gulp, I was yet a contented colossal who'd agreed not to step on anyone, to break ceilings or walls or the backs of bridges or squalling men, as long as I was fed, watered, and spoiled.

I settled into my chair, yes, not unlike Mr. Coughlan's chair upstairs really, a relic, too. I had almost as little furniture as he did, as little clutter, yet today there was not enough space in here, either. Still drinking, eating, my hands a mess, my tongue thick and purpled from the wine, I went to the window. Outside white pear-tree petals flurried in the day's breath, I wanted to laugh out loud at myself but more than that I wanted to catch the white bits in my mouth. I leaned out the window, face up to the sky. When was it that I could hear her? Was my mouth already open, catching more than it bargained for, just as the sounds above me formed into something hard and undeniable, that when pitched at my head woke me?

"Hit me," Hope cried. "Now!" Then a scream that tightened the skin on my body. "Do it again!" she commanded.

And I became small again like that, so small I do not know how I swallowed the last of what was in my mouth or gathered the strength to leave my apartment with the intention of stopping it and stopping her.

Music met me as I climbed the stairs. A cover newly thrown over the couple. I knocked. I rang the bell. But the music percussed and shouted; it absorbed everything. I leaned into the bell again, as long as I could to put off, moments longer, opening the door that I guessed would not be locked. My hand was on the knob. I had only persuaded myself to turn it; it felt inert, a brick in the hand; but then it flew away, was pulled from me, and he became the door—Les as molten and obstructing as the first time I saw him.

His eyes flew over my head, narrowed, and he leaned his torso into the hall just perceptibly as if looking first for an adversary, a body roughly his size. He blinked before he lowered his gaze to me, blinked again, then sniffed as if he was not certain that who and what he was seeing was me. Then he hunched over me, and smiled slowly the smile of having discovered a practical joke, one he'd puzzled out before it could harm or humble him. He smiled like I was a woman swatting at gods, and then he sighed, and on his breath came whiskey and pot and the high tide of a woman's sex. I stepped back, he stepped forward.

"It has to stop," I said.

"What?" The music surrounded us.

"It has to stop," I called over it.

"What does?"

"What you two are doing."

He drew the door closed behind him to fend off the music's volume. He returned to face me as he ran his great hand through his hair, pushing it into form. Red knitted through the whites of his eyes; his pupils were overlarge and blunted. He looked again somewhere above and beyond me, his focus going, and then striking on a notion that appeared to delight him, he found my face again and offered, "But we are consenting adults." He was drunk. He was stoned. Behind him, the music ended.

In the new silence, I said, "I'll call the police."

His oxford shirt was not buttoned fully or correctly. His feet were bare. His belt was unfastened under his untucked shirt, his fly half-zipped. He drove his hands into his pockets, as I'd seen him do before. A default position for him. He was trying to compose himself.

"I don't think you will."

"Try me."

Another slow-forming smile. He moved back into the apartment, opening the door wide behind him. "Tell her. Come in and tell her."

His smile vanished as he watched me.

I took two steps toward him.

I stood on the threshold.

She was in a costume that trussed, crisscrossed, and bisected. A woman turned into parts, done up in black—black garters, held up with black straps, a black collar of some sort around her neck. *Porn fantasia.* She'd not been up to returning his gifts after all, and now she leaned to face the only wall that did not house bookshelves, bracing herself against it, legs spread. Her skin was mottled a startled pink on the exposed cheeks of her rear and down the lengths of her thighs. Her back where it was bare glistened with sweat and/or saliva and showed hand marks. Her arms above her head appeared thin and a shocking pale against the rest, the blood leaving them to travel elsewhere, to evidence of the alarm and heat of so much friction and more. The fury of her skin. "Come on, *babeeee,*" she intoned. "Where did you go . . . ?" Her head lolled forward and hung. I could not see her face. She breathed in and called just above a whisper, "I'm cold. I'm so cold."

She was miles gone inside herself and the scenario they'd been playing at; for all useful purposes, she was blind. "Baby, baby, *babeeee,*" she hummed.

I made to go.

He pursued me, my back to him. "She told me about you," he said, "that you're a fighter."

In the hall, steps away from him, I came to a standstill, deciding, trying to decide.

"Beautiful and a fighter."

"I don't like you here."

"She does."

"She doesn't know up from down."

"If I go, she does. You want that?"

My extremities, particularly my hands, started to twitch

with the adrenaline that had found them again. I caught them, knotted them in front of me, held on to them; if I turned around, they would lunge for him.

"Goodbye, fighter." He shut the door, locked it. Music broke out again—as suddenly as laughter might.

Once behind my own bolted door, it was a torch song that came swelling through their floorboards, my ceiling. That was what he'd decided they'd play to now, as they found new positions or so I gathered from the thuds. Then the thrashing, to the round tones of a crooning voice. A standard with a bouncy bass. (Nightmares, waking or sleeping, are made of this sort of incongruity—of pieces that don't, and shouldn't, be fitted together.)

Under my door awaiting me, I'm not sure how long, was a pamphlet on PCBs and animal fat. Angie was recycling her causes; I'd seen this one before; still it was a vestige of a world, the world of this building that I had understood, that had since been altered.

Also on my floor—passed under the door and unseen by me earlier—a note on the back of an opened envelope: "I was here—Marina." Had she cleaned or simply wanted to see me, letting herself in with the key I'd given her? I had forgotten to return her call.

I washed my hands, put my groceries away and out of sight. Corked the wine, wiped the counter.

I took a milk glass of whiskey to my bed. It was Tony

Bennett, I think, singing to them, me. *In other words, I'm yours.*

It occurred to me to leave, but I couldn't; I wouldn't be forced out of what was mine, even as my bed rolled with them. I stood, swallowed a mouthful of whiskey, and turned the bedside radio on. NPR reported on antibacterial products, how some experts maintained they were a detriment to the function and development of healthy immune systems in children. "Overkill," someone said. "Next up we'll talk to our commentators about the Geneva Convention and Guantanamo Bay." I switched to a classical music station—cellos huffing low and long—and got up to lie down on the oak of the floor, as far from them above me as I could get; the wood was cool against everything overheating in me. Above me now: *Yes, it's only a canvas sky, hanging over a muslin tree* along with gleeful horns and was it? Yes, scatting. *C'mon, baby. We can't.* My husband that day. Hollow as a barrel.

I crawled partially under my bed. An island of dust there and a lone paperback, a Signet edition of *Moby-Dick.* I had several editions. His. Ours. Mine. But I always kept one within reach. A trick. To time travel. I held the book to me, smelled it, and tried to piece passages together from memory. The soliloquies came easiest—some ridiculous if taken out of context. My resplendently healthy husband reading to me, alive and laughing with amazement at Ahab's address to the head of a dead sperm whale: "Speak, thou vast and venerable head, which, though ungarnished with a beard"—*Celia! Ungarnished with a beard?! Can you believe this guy?*—"yet here and there lookest hoary with mosses; speak, mighty head, and tell us the secret thing that is in thee." I had known this bit by heart for so long, as well as the next lines: "That head upon which the upper sun now gleams, has moved amid this world's foundations—" *Moved amid the world's foundations? I mean, this guy was fearless!* I checked myself against the dog-eared page, touched each line: "Thou hast been where bell or diver never went . . . Thou saw'st the locked lovers when leaping from their flaming ship; heart to heart they sank beneath the exulting wave; true to each other, when heaven seemed false to them . . ." Melville's captain calling to the carcass as if it were an oracle. My husband reading those long, propulsive sentences with the thrilled breathlessness Melville hoped for. The author's daring. His excess and live fancy set against such homeliness, all the minutiae of whale fishery and functions of the blood. *You like the gore, baby.* It was true.

On another dog-eared page, I read to myself: "In most land animals there are certain valves or flood-gates in many of their veins, whereby when wounded, the blood is in some degree at least instantly shut off in certain directions. Not so with a whale; one of whose particularities it is, to have an entire non-valvular structure of the blood-vessels, so that when pierced even by so small a point as a harpoon, a deadly drain is at once begun upon his whole arterial system . . . Yet so vast is the quantity of blood in him, and so distant and numerous its interior fountains, that he will keep thus bleeding and bleeding for a considerable period; even as in a drought a river will flow, whose source is in the well-springs of far-off and undiscernible hills." The wonder at it—the author's, my husband's, mine, how even in the details, yes, of the gore I'd come to love then, he is looking for mystery, for God or gods; Melville was extravagant. My husband loved him for that, how the reader was necessarily lifted off the page, up and out of time.

A howl from upstairs. Unmistakable delight in it. I covered my ears. I shut my eyes and saw Starbuck confronting Ahab in his cabin. "The oil in the hold is leaking, Sir." I didn't need the page; I recalled Starbuck's urging, though, admittedly, in my husband's excited voice: "We must up the Burtons and *break out*," yes, before all the oil on which the owners of the ship were depending was lost. Ahab nearly shoots Starbuck at the suggestion; it meant they'd have to pause in their hunt for the whale. Ahab rails, sends Starbuck off, but then in a remarkable turn, just after the first mate is gone, Ahab relents. Like that. Ahab's passion needing Starbuck's pragmatism, needing reprieve from a goal so driving and depleting, needing to gather the steadier breath back to him long enough to query what is worth saving? What is worth chasing? What is real?

Les had called me beautiful. He couldn't have known that no one did anymore, nor did I want that word from anyone except someone who had given it to me in a way I understood—who liked to encounter and re-encounter even the skin in so slight and forgotten a spot as my earlobe. I held my earlobe between my thumb and index finger now. It was the skin just there, the tiny pulse; before he became too ill, it could begin there between us, depending on his mood. At any given time I had been a woman whose neck was knotted, whose hair probably needed a washing, whose feet hurt from shoes not designed for her comfort, but wherever he touched me, I could not help imagining something delicate against everything hewn and rough around it. Everywhere along the Maine coast he loved, there were crowds of sea roses. I could not help but think of them— those sturdy roses. In Vacationland. His salt in my mouth, his tongue. *C'mon, baby, let me in.* Soon I was made of those seaside petals; his own skin and body waking and warming, as mine began to turn, to give way. He lifted my hips and cradled my lower back, making it feel at once small and as expansive as sky, and then making it vanish into his touching me, his hands that knew where to go on me, when to wait and when to forget waiting, to forget himself. His lips and teeth mapped the last of my skin on the back of my neck—yes, there, one of the places my nerves always called to the rest of me most emphatically, that sent live threads to my toes and heart, fingertips *and* stomach until toes, fingers, and more dissolved, too. *My beautiful.* His word, his possessive. Not beautiful girl or wife or woman, no domesticated adjectives, but his simple descriptor, more timeless, at least to me, breaking time even now. *Let me in.* Yes, I was no longer reducible to parts. I was no longer merely female. I was alive under him, coursing and losing surfaces to sensation: my breasts just breasts before the lines everywhere tense and electric inside me claimed them too, and as his mouth pulled on them, the communication of lines pulled me into them and into feeling. Between my legs, he ran fingers between lips, inside inside-lips, *for me,* reminding me of the contours going liquid there, of all the ways I could know them and them me, not for theater, but because they were mine and he loved what was mine. And so he could be my strength, the hard part of me, inside me, riding the coursing and the melting and the pounding—of his body and mine, yes, but especially of blood—his blood and mine under skin that was no longer skin. So much blood between us. *My beautiful.* Eyes closed. Eyes opened. It did not matter because either way he was all through me, even his voice reddening in my veins, and I was everywhere him, a body turned inside out for him because he had loved what was mine. I remembered. Yes, he loved what was mine.

HELPING HANDS

—

I HADN'T REALLY WOKEN or perhaps I was barely awake. I moved through the morning's rituals and requirements; my husband's hands following me, caressing me, as I dressed. Some days, not as many as I would have liked, I could have him back. For a few hours or longer, I could see myself through his eyes, feel myself humming as he'd made me hum, feel held in his regard. And however long it lasted, this sensation, it was more dramatic than anything else around me. In here. Why shouldn't my past, as I'd known it to the detail, be as real as anything else? As habitable? Didn't I owe him that?

When my bell rang, I doubted it, didn't care to hear it. When it rang again, I put my back to it, ran my fingers through my hair, and stirred a density of ambered honey into my tea. The third time it sounded I saw Mr. Coughlan's face and then wondered about the temperature outside. It was yet a cold spring. I set my tea down and worked the intercom. The voice, one I'd heard before, issued statements: "Detective Brazo. Here about a missing persons complaint."

I hesitated.

"Hello?" he called through the box of wires. "This is the NYPD. I'm looking for the landlady, a Celia—"

I buzzed him in. Too quickly was he at my door. I opened it but stood in the frame. I rarely allowed anyone in my place, and now here was a man who smiled just as readily as Les had, at something as flimsy as a woman alone.

"Are you—?"

"I am the landlady here."

He told me my name again. I nodded. More establishing facts. "Mr. Coughlan's your tenant." I nodded again and again. Because I didn't move aside, he smiled less and less. A silence hovered, landed. "Can I come in?"

Did he have to? Would he think it, me, suspicious? Did it matter what he thought? I expected the police at my door before. I would have welcomed them. But now? I was better defended. I had practice.

"Sure." I shrugged; oh, but I moved aside with well-broadcast reluctance as he pulsed past me and roamed feet from me; a wiry man, it appeared, with the city all through him. He had a long bone of a nose on a short face, a smallish cleft chin, a profusion of eyebrows, bouncing with the roaming of his eyes, looking for anything, everything. I tried not to see so much, not today, not the wave in his thick hair or his sun-loving skin and the wide pores there, or the day-old beard coming in that was a field of hard black pushing and pushing. . . . But I always had—gathered details to me, even the ones I did not want, so many—and in the last five years the tendency had only increased. I did not enjoy visitors, and unexpected visitors, unless it was Marina or her family, felt particularly unkind.

"You look familiar," he said, eyes and brows running away from me, around the room.

"Huh."

"You moving in or moving out?"

"No."

He eyed me, from my feet up this time. "Which one?"

"Neither. I like to keep things spare."

"This Jeanette Coughlan, the daughter, is no fan of yours. She thinks you're involved in her father's disappearance." He held himself as motionless as he could to see if I'd react.

"Involved is one thing I am not."

He mistook the comment for levity, flirting. "*Really?*" His eyebrows climbed.

I knocked them down, crossed my arms over my chest: "No, I mean, I believe in privacy, respecting it."

"She thinks you're taking his money."

"I've taken some. The rent every month." I did not tell him that Mr. Coughlan hadn't paid the rent consistently in a year or so. I did not tell him I did not care whether he paid or not, or not in some time. Perhaps I should have explained, but I needed my privacy, at that moment more than ever.

He pulled out a sad-looking notebook, and we traveled more facts: How long had he been renting here? Four years. How long since I'd last seen Mr. Coughlan? Two weeks. How would you describe your relationship? Cordial. Rent—how much? Below market. Any disputes in the building? None. I gave only what the detective asked for because I couldn't give more—I so wanted him to go.

"Will you excuse me for a moment?" I asked.

I made for the bathroom, tried not to run. I plucked at the bottles in the cabinet, decided on Xanax, this one prescribed to me, and represcribed, since expired, yes, but not long ago. Only months. Here and there I had needed help to sleep, to relax. I'd been confident I didn't need more. Or rarely. I sucked on the bitterness of the pill as I sat on the toilet and imagined my husband's strong hands holding my rib cage, to steady my breathing, my heart.

I had felt the rainbow of my husband's body, his everything, awake and asleep. All night I had sunk back into him, and he'd let me. And all morning while drifting and dreaming him, I had listened to public radio's Saturday early show, to their version of the world—books, sports, politics; a conversation with a guitarist whose fingers found the songs for him, with a novelist who believed the novel dead, with a Republican congressman turned Democrat turned Republican.

Now, here, these people kept coming. Hope. Mr. Coughlan. His daughter. A policeman. Years later. Upstairs more news from worlds that should not be bearing down on my own. *These people.* I have not harmed them. I wouldn't or not intentionally. That was never the idea. To harm anyone. When the taste became too much, I drank from the faucet to chase the pill down my throat. I breathed in, out.

"Everything okay in there, ma'am?"

These people.

"Yes."

I emerged to his roaming eyes. "A little under the weather," I told him.

"Stomach thing?"

"Would you like to see his place? Mr. Coughlan's?" I rummaged in a drawer of keys in a credenza by the door. "Top floor." I placed my hand on my stomach. "I hope you won't mind if I don't join you."

He shifted from foot to foot, deciding whether to go alone. His brown jacket sleeves were too long and his blue pants shone from too many visits to the dry cleaner's. His Adam's apple was so sharp it looked like it would hurt to touch it.

"I'll come back after I've looked around."

"Fine," I said. "Great."

"You'll be here?"

"Yes."

He turned to go. Turned back. "Are you sure we haven't met?" His breath smelled of mustard.

"I'm sure."

I locked the door behind him, put my hand on it to ask it to stay, to protect me as well as it might. I thought of my husband's hand on the Brooklyn Bridge stanchion, thanking it, comforting it. His imagination extending to everything alive and inanimate.

I flushed another pill into me, choosing for color, another color, this time pale green, and I called my husband to bed and waited for the medicine's effects and the sensation of heat, his, to come and climb my spine. What is better than a solid, willing man lying behind you, cupping his body around yours? In no hurry. Forgetting time. One person stacked securely into the other. When my husband passed, at first, I couldn't be inside and wandered outside too much, the whole of me an open mouth, an open pair of arms. My welfare scarcely an afterthought. Then I wouldn't go out or rarely. I had scared myself into seclusion. I avoided friends or they, increasingly, avoided me. I saw doctors who enumerated the stages of grief, of trauma—as if the predictability of emotions should provide succor. No one asked me about his last day. No one cared to. They handed me slips for the pharmacy. To and from the Rite Aid I passed a Realtor's office, and there, photographed, was the façade of my building—brownstone, which is of course brown hard stone. Resilient old Brooklyn replete with its own stories, but how slender and unassuming this building looked compared to its neighbors, more durable than grand, yes. I arranged to see it, bought it, moved, and asked myself for courage. I took enough medicine to help me sleep and walked every morning. In the light. My portion of it. My share, learning if not to like then to abide my own company again. *I tried not to look for you on the streets or in other men's bodies. They were my punishment for finding myself so alone. Oh, darling, darling. Here I am now.* A chill of joy at feeling something remarkably like his full, hot breath on the back of my neck. The drugs began to subdue and widen the currents in me. Yes, I took them as little as possible because after they wore off, often, there was a price; the world lost all its vividness for a time, but today they gave me the richness and possibility of my own company, and his, which I could conjure as lushly and fully as I needed. In less than an instant, my tenants struck me as cartoons, then became shadows, as I led him to touch all the places in me that most needed to be touched. I was cherished in my bed by me, by him, by memory. I fell into an exhilarated state, part sleep, part charge in my lungs. "You can have all this and more," he said, confiding, filling my ear. "What is more?" I asked him. He didn't answer. "What is more? More of you?" I asked again as knocking came. It sounded from miles away. Across distance. More knocking. I got up to address it. I'd managed to forget the policeman.

"Ah, you're back," I said.

His mouth and hands flew. He went at a speed I could not fathom now, that seemed comic. Another cartoon. This was the police? Law and order?

"I figured out where I've seen you. Helping Hands. You work there?"

"I volunteer." Yes, I had given much away when I moved, much of my own wardrobe, but there was an Irish sweater of my husband's I'd included in the donations by mistake. I went back in tears, and I was led to piles as big as me, to search and sift until I found it, through hundreds of sweaters discarded, homeless, now unbelongings, and somehow comforting, as were the women in charge of the piles. They chatted, laughed, as they sorted with gloved hands. They understood duty as I did and chose their own pace, were kind, and so I went back for their fellowship and to be reminded how we let go, if we can, and in what vast quantities. Mountains of unbelonging.

"My wife—we're separated—she takes stuff there religiously. She *is* religious. She likes Jesus a lot better than she does me. Can't say I blame her."

I was supposed to laugh here so I did. My face loosened in front of him, the rest of the taut strings in me loosening too. My knees laughing even. I braced myself against the credenza by the door. I laughed longer than I should have.

"Who writes on the soup?" he asked.

"Soup?" What a strange word that was and how right it seemed then—soup, a warm marsh. I was soup. Who could write in soup?

"His daughter?" he asked.

"Oh, yes, maybe," I said, though I immediately doubted it.

"The writing looks a lot like the writing on the mailboxes in the entry hall. I took that to be your handwriting."

"Oh, yes, I'm sorry. The cans, you mean? On them? Yes, yes, it is mine." I nearly giggled. This was the police? Finding me out? Pursuing the soup-can writer? Years too late.

"Are you okay?"

"I'm better. I was lying down. I'm just, you know"—I smiled into his eyes, hoping to hold on to them and those bouncing eyebrows—"out of it, pooped, really."

"So you write on the cans?"

"I date them. I want to make sure he eats."

"Does anybody know this?"

"You and me." I pointed to him, then to me, feeling a savage silliness. "You and me."

He stepped closer to me, smiling again, breathing his mustard at me. "Do you buy the soup?"

"I replace the soup when it needs replacing. Simple as

that. I lock his door when he forgets. I throw out the sour milk. I buy more milk."

"That's nice."

"I'm not . . . nice." I meant to say something about duty, responsibility, but I couldn't get it out of me fast enough.

"I think you *are* nice." He straightened up, put his hands in his pockets, became expansive to prepare for his speech. "I think some people don't expect people to get them. I think you've been alone a long time and have gotten used to it." His Adam's apple rolled and pointed. "I won't argue with you about that, right? Not my business, though maybe it's a shame, you know? Maybe. Maybe not. Hey, don't let me overstep here. But I think Mr. Coughlan's daughter and probably everyone has got you all wrong."

The detective looked proud of himself, with his flashing face and unmoving hair. Who was everyone, I wanted to ask but didn't. I couldn't locate the words in the warm marsh.

"I knocked on a few doors. One place. Nobody home. At this hour, I expected as much. But another apartment, a lady answered the door—a Hope something? And some tall guy coming out quick to check me out, you know? Sure. They asked if you called about noise. I told them, no such thing—" He went on, and I saw Les as a wall again, fending off this odd character with his sad-looking notebook, building his assumptions, and Hope walled in. Hope in costume. Hope without hope.

How suggestible I was and suddenly how weary. Hope and Les stood on my shoulders. I held on to the credenza. *These people.* The detective had to go now; before he did, I had to say one more thing: "I went looking for him, Mr. Coughlan. He was seen at Whitehall, at the terminal there, a week or so ago. He rode the ferry back and forth, chatted the men up. A man named Frank saw him, and someone else did too—a Billy or Bobby. They tell me he's fine. I don't know, but they say a man like him needs—"

"A regular Nancy."

"Did you say Nancy?"

"Nancy Drew." He laughed.

"No, no, air, and I'm . . . I was—" I could barely stand. I saw Hope with her back to me, giving me the pink of her flanks. That music from last night, played too loud, surely in part for me, because of me. Fatigue reduced me; I knew only two things: I had to sleep, and I had to ask Hope to leave my building as soon as I could. "I try not to involve myself," I said to the detective and to Hope. "But it is so important that we all respect each other's—"

"Space." The detective peered into my face. "You really don't look so good. You're dead on your feet. Something you ate? A bug?"

"I am just so tired . . ."

His mouth made the smallest of talk, too small to follow. *Old man, his age,* he said. *Why hasn't he come home? He's vulnerable, sure. Anything could have happened between then and now or maybe not . . . I'll check it all out.* I leaned into the credenza and away from his talk of new risks to my tenant. The pale green pill was a sedative. I whispered, "I'm not so strong." He didn't hear me; he was going of his own momentum now, a man full of purpose, show, and back in my bed, the sheets having turned cold, in full daylight, I tumbled and went out.

AWAY INTO ANOTHER
WOMAN, ANOTHER MAN

———

WHERE I WENT, I couldn't say. Where I returned I did not recognize at first. I smelled Pine-Sol and had to keep blinking to make out the time on a clock I didn't believe in. I lay there debating every thing around me, even the daylight and a terrible absence that made even the empty air around me too full. The danger of suspending reality or your more banal agreements with it was that you couldn't call it back when you chose. It had to be courted, wooed. It took work. I knew the regimen: A shower, caffeine, the sun full in your eyes if you could get it, all this helped, but above all you had to be willing to make new agreements and to keep moving without thinking too much, to see and register the world around you for its absolute surfaces, for its mute particulars, without resistance or much internal conversation, and especially without longing for something else.

I saw numbers indicating 1:30 in the afternoon become 2:30 before I decided I was willing to move. But my body remembered better than anything conscious in me the sweetness of what had been restored to me, and it dragged behind my directives to wash and drink black tea into what I had finally agreed, yes, was afternoon. My body's reluctance stood me before a mirror to look at it after I'd showered; I wore my husband's eyes to study my body as he did, the unblemished white of it, the leanness, the length of my neck. A body that was neither young nor old, though I could see textures in the skin across my stomach and over my knees that hadn't been there before and different contours along muscles in my arms, new hollows, and that my hips and breasts were fuller, the lines of my jaw and nose sharper. Cold traveling from my feet standing on the uncovered floor nearly drove me back to bed, but I shook it off and at my bureau dutifully found underwear, a bra, and in that same drawer, barely buried, a note I'd taken from the Braunsteins' apartment: *I'll wait for you* in a stranger's hand. I stared and stared at it, as I had the clock, waiting for it to make sense of itself, why I'd taken it. All that I could come up with, agree to, as I dressed, was that it shouldn't be here any longer.

I made myself presentable and approached my door. It required a few attempts and one trip to the medicine cabinet before I made it out. I placed one pill, an ancient yellow Klonopin, in my windbreaker pocket, as a companion, a sort of encouraging talisman, nothing more. Backup I wouldn't need.

I exited to clean hall floors. Marina had been here—used the Pine-Sol she and I had agreed to years ago. If she'd come knocking or ringing, I'd been insensate. The stillness in the halls told me she was gone now. No one was about.

Absence again, widening and widening before me. I hurried past it to the front door and flung myself outside.

But the day ran too high. It was radiant and boasting, making a parade of its assets and so required cheering bodies and attitudes. The birds screamed. I stepped back inside. In the empty halls, scrubbed nearly to sterility by a Marina so starkly gone, the building did not breathe. Beside my own, it seemed to have no human breath in it at all. It felt sealed, even to me. A distortion maybe, one of any number I'd left myself open to by needing ghosts and going away as I had, part of the cost, but one I could not brook for long if I meant to decipher between what was safe in these walls and what was not.

I got all my keys. I took the elevator. There was nothing to remark inside it; it seemed impossible that anything untoward had ever happened in it. At Mr. Coughlan's door, I knocked as a formality, part of the work, the means of meeting superficies. On the other side nothing moved, nothing could. I touched every piece of his furniture. New

York dust of streets and bodies and traffic and buildings had settled on everything already. The city shedding even here, in empty rooms. In his fridge, mold had taken over most of the cheese and bread. I left them for now. I didn't want to argue or fuss. My job was to see what was; that he'd never meant to stay long; that the rooms meant nothing to him—just the solitude they offered and that view of the harbor.

At the Braunstein door, I knocked harder and repeatedly. When I opened the door, I called, "It's Celia. I smelled gas in the hall." And I proceeded in: "Anybody home? Hello? Hello? So sorry to intrude—" The paint cans had been stored away or disposed of; the furniture and lamps were restored. The colors Angie had newly applied were just as glaring as on my last visit, but the odd tidiness of the place now, the fact that all the wall hangings, the masks, and more were not yet rehung but stacked to face a corner, seemed a chastisement as if some life or quality of home was now to be withheld.

In the kitchen the surfaces were bare and faultlessly clean. Wasn't the absence of Angie's militantly healthy products, and her pamphlets, equal to her own absence?

In the bedroom, I discovered the cause—Mitchell's things were gone. The tapestry over the bed, even the photo on the bureau that recorded a man in love's compliance, had all been removed, making the room at once bigger and smaller. I opened the bureau drawers. Angie's underwear was uniformly cotton, plain and white with only one interruption of something more conspicuous. I dug for what I found was a lace DayGlo fuchsia thong, and then hit something else, what looked like a lavender compact. I popped it open. Beige birth control pills arranged in a tidy circle. She'd already taken today's dose. Angie? Who decried chemicals in the environment manipulated her own body's?

I opened another drawer and felt through her no-frills bras, another drawer of her sloganed T-shirts, her jeans. Just Angie. I had the note I'd taken in my pocket still. I had nowhere to return it now with the closet emptied of Mitchell.

How hastily these rooms could alter with their occupants and how much they took when they left. Mitchell had taken some of her color, her boldness, and now the light in the bedroom surging through the southwestern windows left nothing to darkness; everything was exposed, including what was sunk into every object and surface here—a sad bewilderment. It found an easy host in me. I did not want it or this note. I went to shove the piece of paper in the bureau under Angie's clothes. It had belonged here, that it did not now could not be my puzzle to suss or work through.

But I couldn't do it. I'd missed my chance.

I left the Braunsteins' with the note still in my pocket.

I recomposed myself at George's door or struggled to—I reconstructed the other night, the indignity of it and Les looming over me. Les claiming where he stood and me backing away. I knocked politely. Yes, yes, even Hope would realize she couldn't stay here any longer. She'd let loose too much of her. A monster in the building, in the halls, and now Mitchell gone, too. Mitchell given up the chase. A disciplined man. A man once so besotted. *I'll wait for you.* I knocked harder. The woman on the Promenade who collapsed into him. She looked the part of someone waiting a long time, biding her days for one person. Willing. Regardless of the cost. The note meant nothing to them now. My knuckles stung. Clearly no one was inside George's apartment, but I'd had to gather my forces. A landlady's poise.

"Hello, hello!" I yelled, as I unlocked the door. I repeated the line about the gas. I did smell something as I walked in, spoiling though not yet rotted food, garbage not yet disposed of. Pillows were scattered on the floor. On almost every table—kitchen, coffee, bedside—a used glass with the smear of lip- and fingerprints visible even at a remove. The kitchen counters housed a jumble of take-out containers, cookie and cracker boxes, a bland brick of aged cheddar cheese and the knife that had stabbed at it, empty vases and bottles—Dewar's, Coke, cranberry juice, Prosecco, tonic. The gardenia was gone; maybe tossed or given away to more competent care?

Even before I entered the bedroom, I could feel the bed sweating and swelling. It was stripped of all its covers so it could not hide and gave off sex in such a musk that one couldn't stop the images of the opening and closing of bodies, mouths, armpits, legs, and suggestions that became impressions in the nose and throat. George's orchids drooped like languid captives against the drawn shade and closed window. Their soil wasn't dry—perhaps it had been, and Hope had overcompensated. I did not know how to cure this, to *un*water, to *un*saturate.

I touched nothing except her journal, which I found again under the bed. She and Les had exploded my privacy without concern so if I had any lingering misgivings about dipping into the book again, they had no real voice in me. On the last recorded page were numbers—a salary with bonuses calculated, the estimated worth of a brownstone, a cottage in Rhinebeck, the value of a two-year-old Subaru, a Mercedes (30,000 miles, *pristine* she'd written and underlined). Millions of dollars tallied and retallied, records prepared, the price of her part in a shared life. She circled a sum and beside it: "How much is mine?" Below that, what I took to be a date of birth and a social security number. Hers? Making her official? And at the bottom of this page in a tight, shrinking script: "I am losing my mind."

I flipped two pages back, away from a list of paintings, silver, place settings, and glassware until I found some continuous sentences in a low long scrawl:

> *I let him dress me up. I don't refuse a thing now. He hits me when I ask for it. He wants to marry me. He thinks this is the stuff of marriage.*
>
> *He keeps talking about a ménage à trois, a kid in a*

candy store, eyes too big for his stomach or his cock. Another
woman. He says, "It will be a trip." Away. Away. Fly away into
another woman—

I found my name on the next page.

Celia!? Must try to speak to her. The police were here.
I half-hoped they'd take us away.

Did Les tell Hope I'd come to them out of concern for
her and was this next line written below the rest, after a
series of ellipses and empty lines, evidence of it?

I am humiliated. And what's worse is that I don't care.

I brought the book to my nose. It smelled of her perfume. At the going-away party for George, I had marveled
at her posture, the sureness of her shoulders. Her perfume
defeating me now, I sat on the bed. I lay back into the slag
of it. It disgusted me and—I could not help it—it titil-
lated me. A trip into another woman, another man. Here
was the longing I'd promised myself to abstain from. I
drank down the bright yellow pill in my pocket with the
remnants of the amber-colored water in a highball glass by
the bed. "My darling, my darling," I whispered, "she has
to go." I knew too much. I'd known it from the first but
let myself be taken in. I drew my hand across the fitted
sheet, then between my legs. I held the book to me with

my other hand. I waited on the medication to open different currents in me, less strange and starved, and easier to follow out of this suffocating place.

Dear George, I hope this letter finds you well. I have missed you. The building has—a bird went off in my ear, an ecstatic pointed call. Somehow I'd made it outside with the sun now driving into my eyes, the spring day's fanfare swirling around me, taking me in and bumping me along as I composed the letter I'd have to send to George to explain, but I couldn't say I missed him, could I? It revealed too much to a man I'd made it my business to reveal little to—as a courtesy. I could say I missed seeing him, yes—and the order of his rooms, his books. A man who thought to collect Colette and Simone de Beauvoir on his shelves as well as Auden and Chesterton; George, a man who never let dust collect or his plants suffer. What had he said? A sensuality of time and landscape that could not be had in America? Maybe so and maybe it could not be had in him while he was here. . . .

I looked to the daffodils and tulips and hyacinth. The tiny plots of soil before the buildings and brownstones along the streets had broken open at last, wishing they were bigger. Within their confines, they ran with color and life, and how I missed George, yes, keenly, within mine. He had kept his dramas close, let the walls between us be walls. Grief carried on too long is a self-indulgence. George had said that to me once. Yes, some weeks after his lover had left him, after he'd paced my ceiling long enough. We don't always have a choice, I told him in reply then. Some things are sacred to us because, well, they are. Did I say that? Words like it, I recall, but I did not go on. Yes, to describe certain things aloud was to give them and yourself away, to cheapen them. My grief was mine. We can claim that about so little, really, especially on a day like this where the world was so alive that it reverberated and re-created at a frantic pace. I continued my letter, *There are certain rules of behavior that are consented to . . .* No, that wasn't right. *Neighbors or good ones . . . Good neighbors shield one another from certain behaviors, from certain choices we cannot help but make. We are not expected to be . . .* What? Perfect? *We are not expected to be without our . . . releases, but perhaps merely mindful . . . mindful of others.*

I sounded like a prig.

The sun blinded me as I followed the sidewalk, so I could not gauge if I'd made sufficient room for others and brushed into someone's shoulder as he or she passed. "I'm so sorry," I said. I used my hand to shield my face, to see an attractive man in his late thirties or early forties. He wore a ragged Rolling Stones T-shirt and had a hard-boned, lately unshaven face, soft shaggy auburn hair.

"Don't worry about it." He grinned fully to his ears. I expected him to rush off, but the day, its volume, possibility breaking over us—"What a day, huh?"

"Oh, yes, the sun. I couldn't see." I grinned back for

him and did not move off as I should have. The pill slowed my common sense, my body, the day. I knew that's all it took at times—an expression on the face, staying in proximity to someone a second or two too long, looking into, really *into,* someone's eyes with feeling—any feeling, it didn't matter which—as he was doing with mine now. I let him. It had been a good while since my eyes played at playing with a strange man's, and then the anti-anxiety medication could turn the course of a day into a series of loose, unhurried queries, the stuff of curiosity and all seemingly harmless, especially today, *today.*

"Hey, can you tell me if there's an Internet café around here somewhere? I need to get online." He tapped his computer bag with his tapered fingers. "I have no connection at the place I'm staying."

There was an invitation: for me to ask where he was staying, to begin the parsing and swapping of personal information, the letting go of priorities or the reshuffling of them. "No, I don't know," and I didn't know and felt foolish suddenly. I was not in the world the way others on these streets were and didn't want to be. I gave my face back to the bright of the sun, stepped back, preparing to set off. "Maybe on Court Street," I said. "Everything seems to be on Court Street." How silly it was, standing in the middle of a day that had so much to do. With a palsied wave, I forced myself to return to George with more concentration this time: *I am sorry, George. I hate to disappoint you. I wanted our building to be a safe place, a quiet place for her.* Isn't that what she had said? A place apart . . . *But she is not well and is making decisions or failing to make decisions* . . . How to say it? That she herself is not safe? . . . *that are jeopardizing* . . . The walls? Yes, she did not respect the walls, had made them so pliant, half liquid, and barely there so that I was forced to see things in her that are better not seen . . . *jeopardizing the privacy that is so necessary in a building like ours, in a city like ours. I simply cannot condone this, George. To do so would mean I do not care and I do. Do not think me cold* . . . Around me the trees shushed in a new gust, and the thousands of fallen petals from those pear and cherry trees, spring's mess, still stuffing up the cracks of the sidewalk and collecting in the gutter moved over-ground puffing briefly into mad little cyclones. *Oh, George, it's so beautiful here now. I wish you could see it. Did I ever tell you my husband wanted to be a writer? But then in New York commerce is so beguiling. It catches you from just about everywhere. Commerce that can't help but attract the most energy and creativity these days, as if dollars were being imagined into existence just for those willing to get in, stay in.* Yes, commerce with its own violent heartbeat, and then the stakes were real for my husband as they had once been for my father. A New York game he wanted to play and win, keep up and claim. He designed programs and applications for traders whose needs were unfailingly immediate. NOW. NOW. NOW. He made money, saved money, yes, but one day when he'd had the outsize success he wanted here, we'd be free. *We intended to live abroad. Turkey. Italy. Maybe even France. Can you imagine such freedom, George? Was it ever possible?*

Footsteps behind me. The man in the T-shirt walked two or so yards behind me and gaining. I'd seen that his pants had hung low enough to reveal the band of his underwear—briefs not boxers on a thin, taut man, veins boasting of his energies all over him. A man who could be out of his clothes in no time. Textures everywhere along the streets we all walked and stories too. Touch one. Choose one, as George had done. *Come to Aarhus in the spring.* Or choose what you cannot help but choose. What nourished you the most. Or what protected you? Yes. That. At whatever the price.

I stopped and whirled round to face the man. "Can I help you?" I asked with a show of impatience.

"You said Court Street, right?"

"Right."

"And that's this way, right?"

"Yes. Yes, of course, it is."

"I didn't mean to bother you." His face had turned grave, his brow lowering and showing an overhang of forehead that suggested the durability of bone. He readjusted his bag on his shoulder. He had lovely hands. I never could keep from noticing hands.

"You didn't. You haven't." Even with the Klonopin numbing and numbing, sweat came out in pins all over the back of my neck. I couldn't move.

"Okay," he said. "Okay," again as a parting gesture and then he passed me as I stood still so that I had to watch him go. Away. Go away.

*I had no other recourse but to ask her to leave, George. She has
resources and so many friends. There are other places for her where
she'll have all that she could want.*

I stood there too long. I did not know where to go,
only that I was not yet prepared to go back to Pacific
Street because when I did I would only be waiting for her
and preparing the right words and tone with which to
make her go. Go away.

I detoured to a nondescript rectangle of a structure of
gray and glass in Metrotech, ribbed inside with vibrating
fluorescent lights. In front, the staff of Helping Hands, a
lesser-known charity in the model of Goodwill, acknowl-
edged me with shadows of smiles and nods—these work-
ers were interchangeable, came and went—but in back
my absence had been remarked by the matrons and main-
stays of the place. These were Ruth, Marla, and Phyllis.
Marla wasn't there today but the other two, older women
both, one a widow, the other long married, teased me,
"We thought you'd run off with a man," but that was all,
and I smiled and shook my head, made up excuses of visiting family and friends, and then listened to them talk of
children and grandchildren, a nephew in Iraq, a sister with
Parkinson's, and to commentary about a television dance
show where that "blond girl," "pretty as a church" looked
"*poor thing,* like she was born without joints that bend" and
how that "big boy" could really "go." "He can eat *and* he
can dance!" While they talked and laughed, our hands
never stopped, separating the good items, many with price

tags, never worn, from the passable, the passable from the irretrievable.

I did not bother to go to my apartment when I returned to Pacific Street. My arms aching, my hands, because I'd forgone gloves, oily from all that had passed through them, other people's things, I went directly to George's door. The day was growing blurred and buttery. I had to try again while I believed in the urgency I felt. I knocked, rehearsing, *I'm not here to judge, Hope. I know what a terrible time it's been for you and your family. But you are exposing—* It was Leo who answered the door. Exhaustion showed on his face, in the low-slungness of his shoulders, and in his composure that was even more uncanny. "Oh, hi," he said as if he'd forgotten me entirely, as if I'd just occurred to him.

"I was hoping I could talk to your mom?"

"Oh, Mom . . . Mom, she's sick. In the hospital." His words were picked and placed side by side more than spoken and for himself first, to persuade himself it was so. I heard him and not—I watched him go still again as he appeared to digest the idea—Mom in the hospital.

"Sick?" I managed to understand. "How sick?"

"Kidney infection, they say. Probably avoidable. I don't think she's been taking very good care of herself. She's on antibiotics. They want to keep her for a day or two."

He ran a hand through his hair, not to smooth it but to

feel it (a gesture so opposite his sister's, one I remembered from our strange tea too full of tensions, that ponytail of the girl's a sort of captivity she'd needed). Under his hand came the sand and oak I'd traced on our first real encounter at my door; and soon the cedar and copper that his body gave off so generously surrounded me. Everything about him seemed always there to be seen and read; he had nothing to hide or if he did, he didn't yet know how.

"No, she hasn't been feeling herself." I nodded and hid my face. It must have had my speech all over it and my disappointment. Nothing would be resolved today.

He straightened and then sniffed as if he'd seized on a concern that had just been out of reach: "She hasn't been, I don't know, creating problems for you, has she?"

"I should talk to her." I forced a smile over my closed lips. "But it can wait," I lied. "There's no real hurry."

I did not know what else to say, and though I should have retreated, my body dug in to be near the smell and open length of him. I should have known better. Only hours ago, I'd misread a man or I'd mistaken my own desire for his. I flushed, blood rushing from my knees up to my face already burning, and even then I did not go. He flushed too, adjusted his shoulders, cleared his throat.

It was a sort of admission from both of us, that we continued to stand there. I hadn't imagined until now that I affected him in any way, that there could be something between us that may have required only nudging. Shy, he had to exhale a reedy breath before he could speak. "You know, I was going to have a drink. A small one. It's been stressful. And then my sister, Danielle—you met her—"

"Yes."

"She's been upset."

"You all have been."

"I appreciated what you did that day when we—"

"I didn't do anything."

He shook his head to dismiss the suggestion. The things he did not know about me, the homeliness I preferred, the simplicity, what in my life, at my age, I'd managed to store and hide and partition, didn't matter against whatever idea he had of me, an idea apparently that moved him. He squinted at me and straightened again. "So that drink?" When I said nothing, he went on, "The place is kind of a mess. I tried to pick up the living room." He looked back over his shoulder, sighed. It wasn't like her, this mess, and he still marveled at it. "Nothing's broken."

Again, his hand went absently to his hair. More than anything suddenly I longed to follow his hand there, get him between my fingers, take Hope's twenty-something son into my arms, lick the cords of his neck and the fullness of his mouth like a calf licks salt. I was hungry and thirsty and so tired of the day and myself, all the effort. And the Klonopin had blunted and cushioned all this till now so that I'd been able to make it outside and into the course of the day and the promise of something new. *Away and into another woman.* Had he seen Hope's journal? Had I put it back where he couldn't see it? I blushed again. My embarrassment volleyed into and burst the cocoon of the last few days. "You can have all this and more"—that line hanging on, lying in wait for me. Was this the more? This unspoiled, defenseless young man in George's apartment? My part in, reward for, this sordid story?

"I'll take a rain check."

I watched him swallow with difficulty. He waited—I waited—until he was ready to say: "When? . . . When can we have a drink?" he asked.

He stepped toward me so I'd have to look at him. He hadn't the right words for what he wanted and was too new to the traffic between men and women, or too alive for pacing himself, for delay. What he had was the desperation and intensity of youth and he wore it all over him and held it there for as long as he could for me to see.

"Not today, but soon," I said and without thinking reached my hand to pat at his arm and offer small, benign reassurance. I didn't expect that he would cover my hand with his and hold it there. I began to breathe unevenly for him to hear as I let him press my palm and all five fingers into him—how long had it been since I touched someone for more than an instant? Hope, yes, her hand as hot as his was now; the blood in mother and son overwhelming and real and as enveloping as flame.

It had to be me who pulled away. Propriety. Yes. How could I ask for it from anyone if I could not give it? But I ached and every bit of me was damp with the ache. It hurt and kept hurting, yes. A cold shower, the efficacy wasn't lost on me, to make me shrink, fit better into the role that was mine here in this building.

I ran the stairs, too aware of how much I'd been running lately when the aim of my life since I settled on this building had been not having to run. The shower first and then the question of failed experiments later. But before I could get behind lock and key, there was my tenant Angie Braunstein on the landing of my floor with all the indications of having waited for me, agitated and pacing with something in her hand.

"Celia! There you are." Such relief in her voice. "I wanted to apologize—I forgot the rent, on the first."

I'd lost track of the dates. I'd not remarked that March was gone. Already gone.

"Oh, yes, Angie. Don't worry. Please don't. I didn't. You're always so conscientious—"

"I've been so—like on another planet—" At that her face reddened, her mole on her full cheek deepening in color. When she handed me the check, folded once in half, her hand trembled.

"Is everything all right?"

"Yes, or well," she paused. "No." And then in what sounded like a series of feigned little coughs, she began to cry. "*No*. No! I don't want to do this! I'm so sorry."

"What is it?"

Her plump, small hands tried to catch her tears. She

looked at me and away, anger brightening her sea-glass-green eyes. "It's— It's—"

My legs felt hollow. My hair stuck to the back of my neck. I formed her husband Mitchell's name, was about to say it for her.

"It's— The polar bears!"

"The *what?*"

"They're dying. So many are already dead. The ice— there isn't enough ice anymore. They can't hunt. They can't get what they need to . . . to . . . live *and* reproduce. They're abandoning—" She started with the little coughs again.

I struggled to prove myself a good student: "Global warming?"

"Yes," she sobbed. "We've been so *selfish*. Selfish! Selfish! Selfish! It's unforgivable, isn't it? I *know* it is. God, *I* know!"

Even as her nose ran and her heavy bosom shuddered, never had she looked more like a doll—a facsimile of a little girl, vulnerable, precious, in need of petting.

"We didn't know," I told her. "We're animals, too, sur-viving. With our own purposes and ideals—"

"No, we've been wrong, *very, very* wrong, Celia," she cried. "All he wanted was a family. To have a family! And I wouldn't—"

"The polar bear?" I asked, to bring her back to me.

She looked at me like I was mad, and then, yes, recov-ered herself enough to say, "No, or yes, the polar bear. I could have done more."

"Maybe," I told her. "But maybe it's bigger than just you and surely it's not too late, Angie, is it?"

She covered her face with her hands.

"It's my fault and I can't stand it, Celia. *I can't!*" She dissolved again and her body shook with violence. I held my face away as I situated my arms around her, elbows locked. I did so less to comfort her than to stem the heaving, to contain her. She would hurt herself.

Hot shower. Bed. As I fell asleep, I drifted with Leo in my arms, then his mother, who he so resembled, then my husband who chased them both away, who stayed and stayed, stayed, who told me again, *C'mon, baby. We shouldn't live like this.* I started a few times, sat up with a terror of the clock and the silence in the room. I saw myself before the medicine cabinet. There was enough in there to send me away, even for good. Of course I'd considered everything, for years now, everything, but no, not tonight. I lay back down, still as a corpse. I had not invited Angie in, though I'm sure she hoped for it. She had soon fallen into me, bucked into my neck and chest with "no's" and tears and snot and the full streaming of her pores. The smell of her upset, the full density of her stout small body and her upset. Angie who I could not say if I liked, ever, in my arms, forgetting propriety. Angie whose belongings I touched, to whom I was sorry and not. What had I told her? We are animals, too, trying to survive? Full of biology's imperatives.

Yes. I could make out the pungency of the oil of her hair. I told it, and her, her name, Angie, *Angie*. It will be all right. *We shouldn't live like this, baby.*

Once she began breathing more steadily, I walked her up the stairs, saw her to her door. A bad day, I told her, trying not to give away the full rough weariness in my voice. A bad day. Sleep it off. It's never too late, I reminded her, though I knew better. She paused. She couldn't go in. I should have asked if she wanted me to come in, but I could not. I was wet with her, my arms, chest, and neck, and knew, again, too much. More perhaps than she did. Yes. The woman on the Promenade, whose vigil was over, whose note it may have or not have been, but then what I most required was Angie's door, which was my door, to swing shut between us. One world effectively separating itself from another. I would not mourn it.

I COULD KILL YOU

―――

THE BANGING INTERRUPTED my father playing the piano and me as a girl listening and wanting, there in our house, for that playing, and the hour in which he played, to draw everything into it.

He would play "Edelweiss" and "Moonlight in Vermont," a sentimental man, especially after an evening drink, unashamed to be so, playing to relax himself away from banking and its politics. I said no or dreamed I did to the noise intruding. I held up my hand. He stumbled on the keys, looked at me with eyes that were also mine, puzzled and faraway, and then the bareness of my room— barer and unfriendlier in the dark—was all around me and with it the recollection, like a slap to rouse me, that my father had always loved my mother more than anyone else, even his daughter with his eyes. I think he was relieved when my husband arrived, and my love for another man floated me away; or maybe not, maybe I had that wrong, but the doorbell serrating into the dark, then the thudding—someone at my door again—wasn't giving me the chance to set it right or give it the fullness of consideration it merited. The glowing digits of my clock reported it wasn't quite 3 A.M. Who would come to me now? It was the dark that brought me all the possibilities—Jeanie Coughlan raging, her father dead, everything my fault. No. I couldn't face that. Maybe Leo had had the drink he proposed to share with me alone, then another. Or worse, an unwelcome ghost from my past. I'd been followed home by one of my subway adventures once. I'd still lived in Brooklyn Heights then. A neighbor had let him into the building. He had waited outside my door, and when I opened it to go out, he'd pushed me back in. He had me flattened beneath him so fast, cursing me, laughing at me, explaining already how our time together would go. He'd made me get up to wash. That was the first time I used the golf club, my father's, given to me as a keepsake. I grabbed it again now.

At 3 A.M. there was rarely good news or a welcome guest, especially with the recklessness in the banging and ringing. Whoever it was had little care for me—even ardor at this hour, so expressed, came as an assault. I gripped the club in my right hand, prepared myself, checked the peephole—a man's Adam's apple right there on the other side, a man with shoulders as full and as impossible to argue with as the side of a barn. Les.

"What do you want?" I called to him. "How did you get in?"

"Where is she?"

"Who?"

"Who else? *Jesus!*" He gave the door a hard jab. "You think you can keep her away from me? Open up! Now!" I peered at him. His hand was still fisted, his knuckles abraded now, just on the other side of my door. Hope must have given him a key.

I tried to calm my voice, my delivery: "Have you been drinking?"

"I can stay out here all night. Tell her to come out! I need to see her."

"She's in the hospital. Leo told me, okay? She's not here, I swear."

"Let me in before I break this fucking door down! I can smell her. I *can*."

"She has a kidney infection. Her son told me. And you should go, Les. Go before I call the police."

Through the peephole I saw his body sway faster and faster, not from disorientation, but to build momentum, as if to a beating of a thousand goading hands on his back.

"You!" he boomed. "You are so full of shit. So full of fucking, fucking shit. *I* am not the problem here. . . . Go ahead and call the police, call them right fucking now. I'll be in there before they've picked up, before they can . . . can . . . fucking . . . *bother* with you. Then we'll see what kind of fighter you are."

It wasn't alcohol or not only—he ran fast and wild and what he imagined was more real to him than anything else. Gratification had to be instant.

"Go home now, you goddamn fool. GO HOME!" I hit my own door. "Do you hear me?"

He threw himself, shoulder first, into my door. Once, then twice. My locks—two deadbolts—didn't give, but the hinges shifted, sifted out dust. I squinted through the hole to see him rear back and do it again, the first time from disbelief, the second from blind animal anger: "Let me in! I need to see her *now*."

Yes, we can't live like this. I dialed 911, reported to the flat inquiry—"What is your emergency"—that someone was working to break down my apartment door, gave my name and address with slow deliberation, interrupting myself to yell at him to *please* lay off, and held the receiver up for them to hear him refuse me: "I'm coming in after her, goddamn you, you goddamn, fucking . . . *obstructionist!*"

I repeated my address, set the phone down.

Leaning into the door again, I could hear his breath beating there. I told him I had called. He backed up again, taking the noise of his chuffing with him. I waited, listened, for his next surge and a sort of groaning, drunken battle cry. He didn't see that I'd opened the door, and so intent was he on his version of things that he didn't see me as he charged in, his eyes fixed on looking only for her. But I saw him, and I struck him on the back of the head as hard and as high as I could with my club.

He went down hands out, reaching for her or for me, or to defend himself against the floor. But once his chest hit the ground, he spread the arms that had already buffered his fall out to either side, as if he were tilting into a bed. He turned his head to one side, then he was out. I stood over him, but he didn't get up, and I could see no evidence of pain on his face or of lungs working. I put down my club, unclenched myself and began to feel the tension in my arms, my jaw, the heat in me receding and a new tide coming in—so cold; the shivering started in my knees, rattling my teeth. And time seemed to seize up for me so that I could feel and hear how much I'd offended: It would stop for as long as I believed I'd killed him.

I had seen dead bodies—my husband's, my father's, a stranger's in a Connecticut coroner's office for the sake of an ambitious AP biology teacher and a good grade. I knew how inert they became, how they cooled and dulled, eyes, skin, lips, how familiar they were as they became something entirely different from animated material like me, yes, like me who could still recall the heat that attended the need—and it was a *need*—to hit him. I wanted him dead as desperately as I wanted an end to all these intrusions, to be master of myself and my property again—all that was there, rigid in my arms, as I had swung up to the back of his head. The weapon I had, my position relative to his, made me as strong as a giant of a man, stronger, and I had relished it. But now I crouched down, sat beside his big unmoving head and made myself as small as I could, knees up to my chest, my arms around my knees, my head buried into them. A host of excuses and revisions and prayers deluged me as I held myself. My mind skittered other places before it circled back to digest what had happened—forming a story. We all are writing and re-writing—so that we might be acceptable to ourselves and others, especially others. Even I was not immune . . . I could not look at him even as I smelled him, the alcohol leaching from him, everywhere. I hated him still, and I had to contain it, me, keep cooling and wishing myself something else, anything or anyone else. But, no, I had to reassemble things. The back of his head before me like a gorgeous, dumb target while he charged like a starved monster. I could not see Les's face, but I could see, as if it had happened today, the face of the man who'd managed to find me at the Brooklyn Heights apartment I'd shared with my husband years ago, which by then had become mine alone. His seething pleasure at having tracked me. Yes, he'd ordered me to wash myself for him—I had to be *fresh as a flower,* he said scornfully. *But you're no flower, are you?* I knew the stock language, the parts assigned. I'd submitted to it before and not merely with him. I went to the bathroom, shut the door, ran the water, and came out to see him sitting on our couch, touching our things, leafing through a pile of our books, the ones I'd kept on hand to read to my husband before he passed: that fairy tale or anti–fairy tale *Lady into Fox,* not yet stored safely away then, C. S. Lewis's *The Screwtape Letters* (which made my husband laugh), poems by Neruda and Sexton (who both understood flesh, its passions and perishability so well), our *Moby-Dick,* the *Odyssey,* and a mystery by P. D. James. I had already planned to go for the club, but outraged I couldn't see and still don't remember the steps to it, to finding it. It was simply in my hands, as if it grew from them, and I held it over him sitting on the couch. I told him I was no flower, no whore, I was no one to him. I explained he was never to come back—when he stood and came at me smiling, thinking this part of the game, I stuck him with the head of the club, straight into his gut. He managed to catch it in his hands, but I was strong then, too, ready to hurt and be hurt, and I ripped it from him and swiped his knees from the side so he'd fall. He did. I stepped on one of his hands, hung over him. "I could kill you," I told him. "I could but I won't. Go away now. If you come back, I will kill you. Whatever you think I am or was, I am not. Do you hear me?" I ground my heel into his hand. "You are not safe here." I pushed the club's head into the back of his neck to force his head down. "Not here," I repeated until he cried out. I moved off his hand.

It felt a miracle when he got up and limped out sniffling and saying nothing. He'd wanted a woman he could dominate—who was willing to let him dominate. Yes, I'd been that woman by choice elsewhere, in the submerged parts of me, on the subway, and if I was led up and out, I was still submerged—so sore was I from mourning. I'd needed to be something else, someone else, but not in my own home and not here, not here. You see, I was no different than Hope, no less a danger to myself and others—I had given myself away, to harm, to unknown appetites— but here, in my own building, I meant to practice life differently, in my way, no one else's.

I brought myself to look at Les. At first I saw nothing, and was confirmed in my fear. I directed myself to blow air into him, to try to resuscitate him with whatever I had in my lungs, and just as I leaned in to turn him over, put his face to mine, he puffed out his lips with a fetid vapor, his dark nostrils opening with it. My hand still shook as I touched his face; it was waxy but warm, blood there, moving under his skin. I'd not been as strong as all that or not stronger than him. I cried then, shaking all over again, this time from joy, and was crying like this, hiccuping, face sweating, nose running, when two uniformed policemen arrived with hands on their guns and eyes twitching. And as I stepped aside to let them in, everything and everyone came with them, time coursing now and making demands—a story. The requisite story in which to package myself, insulate myself from them, a story arranged in an order but not too orderly, with only so many details and those chosen with care. I kept my arms wrapped around my chest, hugging myself, hugging my relief to me to help me, keep me safe, as I asked them first *please* to call the paramedics. *Please, hurry.* He was trying to break the door down, you see, and when I opened the door for fear he'd hurt himself, he threatened to kill me. I had to defend myself. I really had no choice. I did not hit him hard, I told them—I wouldn't. *I'm not that strong, not given to violence. . . . But I didn't have to, you see, he was so drunk or stoned or, god, I just don't know what. Such a big man. So very scary.* I almost laughed when I said it. *I'm all alone here, you see. A widow.*

I lived inside that story for hours into days. I told them I wouldn't press charges, though I fully understood that he might opt to. I worried aloud about how tricky head injuries could be. He hadn't meant harm, had he? He was not himself. I gave the officers the club before they asked for it. I handed it over as if it were the troublesome piece and looked away from it as if it had disappointed me. When they took me to the station to make a statement, they gave me tissues and water in a paper cup, and before we got in too deep, I asked for Detective Brazo. This prompted some surprise. I did not elaborate how I knew Brazo and they did not ask. They simply double-checked to see if I had a record.

Brazo wasn't there at that hour, too late and too early,

but he called the next day and when he did I asked if he would intervene. Les was under the influence or influences, and I had been unreasonably afraid.

"Who wouldn't be?" Angie Braunstein snorted at me, appearing at my door the next day, my champion now. She'd heard the yelling that night. She'd come out to the hall—not sleeping. No one slept much in my building anymore. (Those of us who remained, anyway.) She'd sidled down the stairs, seen the paramedics take Les away, seen me leave flanked by the officers and their obligations to procedure, their youth. "What's going on? What the hell is going on?" she called to us. Les snored on the stretcher, which put everyone at ease and made the paramedics snicker softly. They'd not been gentle with him. They'd moved the tall man like oversized luggage.

"What's going on here?" Angie insisted from the top of the stairs again, and I said, "There's been a little incident."

"Where are you going?"

"Not far. Not far."

And I didn't. At the station, under the fluorescents at 3:30 and 4 A.M., they all relaxed into my version of things. The officers and the desk detective joked about the club being a Calloway. "Not too heavy a feel, for an old driver," said the lankier and more reserved of the two young officers. "Good club."

"Lucky for him," said the shorter and wider of the two, the one who couldn't stop fidgeting with his belt, who'd frowned at me back at my apartment, who'd been so suspicious. "Man, the guy was huge. Center at the Garden huge."

Then, playing my part, I said it, "He wasn't himself."

Brazo said on the phone the next day, "I met that guy, right? The touchy type from upstairs?"

"A friend of one of my tenants."

"I always say neighborhoods don't matter as much as the characters in them. And that guy was trouble looking for trouble."

I protested but not much. Les was in the hospital while Hope was. Trouble looking for trouble.

Different hospitals, the same. I didn't know.

"That's my father's club. Do you think I'll get it back?"

"I'll make it my business to get it to you."

I asked after Mr. Coughlan, but from the distance of the story in which I lived, I could not afford to lose focus too much, to forget a detail, that, for instance, I had been frightened when I hit Les instead of what I was—enraged.

"Yeah, I've been tracking Coughlan."

"So you think he's okay?"

"What he is is on the move."

"Will he come home?"

"Well, to be honest, I'm not sure he knows where that is."

I didn't pursue this or look for fault or tragedy in the reply. I couldn't. What I knew that the detective did not was that there was no chance Mr. Coughlan would come home whole or in pieces while the building was in the state it was in. George had opened a door and let someone in as he let himself out, for more, better, and then a jagged physics took over with the spring egging it on, tossing human appetite in with the copses, in changeable wind and growth so vivid it could barely be believed. If Hope would go, I might have some say. I might have him back. It was not a reasonable supposition but one I could not shake.

I waited and recited my story over and over; everything held in the wait and the telling.

THE SCRIPT

—

MARINA CAME. WE TALKED as I followed her through her cleaning, the tying of her dark and graying hair away from her face, away from work, the unrushed sweeping of her thick ruddy arms over the floor. She asked, as she scrubbed so rhythmically, if her boy could be employed by me. They needed money—more money, she stipulated. Mesmerized, I said, *Sure,* then, *let me think about it.* There was the roof to be repaired. Other things. An old building . . . Always so much to do but not quite yet. We had to wait, though I didn't say this out loud. She looked less sure, less sturdy, Marina did, but I told her my story—of the new tenant and her lover. How he'd threatened to kill me when he had not. I told her how horribly I felt for having to hit him when I did not. "But there was no choice there. Women must defend," she said in her Ukrainian English. And I loved her then and wanted to hug her and let go into the sweat and Pine-Sol stickiness of her as Angie had into me, but I did not. I simply agreed and paid her in advance. I thanked her for coming and asked that she do so as regularly as she could. For the first time ever, because I was shocked to feel the rush of my affection, of my need, I said, "Marina, you must call when you can't come, the day before or, if you have to, the day of. You must give me notice and you must then make up the time. Come another day. Do you understand? If I am to depend on you? Or your son? I'd like that. I do the cleaning when you're not here, but I'd rather you were here doing it." She nodded at me before she murmured, *Of course.* I could feel her marveling at me as I looked away and into my story: *I am all alone here. A widow.* Then she squeezed my wrist as Hope had once done—to show agreement or that she understood or maybe to apologize for not observing our relationship better. I had rarely confided in her and my demands had been few. I had not asked much of anyone since my husband died and now that everything seemed to be asking so much of me, never leaving me alone, I had to be alert. I had to keep score better, draw visible lines.

I did not swallow a pill or sleep well or very long for days. Yes, I waited for Hope, but at night I also waited for Les, Mr. Coughlan, my husband.

I went up to the storage space beside Mr. Coughlan's

empty apartment. I selected a few books from my, our, past. A few movies, old, yet on video. Part of a collection I rotated and varied, restricted my access to. This was how I remembered. Remembered so well. Keeping some things close, others out of reach, alternating. It took practice. Discipline.

I got my mother on the phone. We made plans to make plans to visit, and she reported on dances and new shoes and movies she'd seen—had I been to the movies lately? I did not tell her about Les. I listened to the stream and bubble of her voice, let myself be taken away into her cadence, how everything could be coaxed into freshness if you kept moving and dancing and buying beautiful things, until I heard footsteps overhead. It wasn't even noon; Hope was back. Hope was home.

At her door, I discovered she was not alone. On the other side of her door, conversation was animated, brisk, designed to create cheer or something in its range.

Her friend Josephina let me in. Josephina in black eyeliner and a long black linen top that cinched under her breasts and hung over a long strait of denim skirt. She composed a white smile of greeting under her big, unmoving ringed eyes—"Ah, hello, the lady of the building," she called to me and the others behind her, Hope and Darren.

"The greeting committee," called Darren, who clapped

his tidy toy soldier's hands and gave off a patina of something newly polished—his closely shaven face, his gel-sheened and neatly combed hair, a crisp white and green plaid shirt, a belt buckle flashing like chrome in the light, and white snakeskin loafers. "Another country heard from to welcome our patient home," he went on, drawing me into their project as facilely as that.

Someone, Leo, I suspected, had made piles—a pile of unshelved books, of pillows and throws, CDs, a row of his mother's unpaired shoes—to one side of the living room in order to attack the task of cleaning it. As part of this he'd sprayed Lysol—a gesture of someone who didn't know the smell, which spoke of public lavatories and neglected waiting rooms, was not worth whatever the stuff's benefits. Or maybe he did know but meant to punish the rooms for what had become of his mother in them.

That woman, uneasy, had situated herself in the middle of George's leather couch, which, thanks to Leo, was naked of pillows and throws and other softening influences. She sat with her back painfully straight, unwilling to give herself to the couch or the room. She looked at me as if she had difficulty focusing her eyes on the figure of me, as if I were too bright or hard to imagine. She looked at me with reluctance. Misgiving, yes. Yet outfitted in a silk pale blue robe, she managed to conjure Lauren Bacall or Rita Hayworth, a woman at a dressing table, pretending to arrange the luxury of her hair, of her. She'd flung off the clothes she'd worn to and from the hospital, surely, and this robe was chosen by her or Josephina to usher her back to a version of herself that merited silk, that liked it against her bare skin; for the material was thin enough to show her body's lines, the forwardness of a nipple, the shape of a rib cage, hips.

I took all of her in—her bare feet, the chipped pink toenail polish, the untidiness of hair held up by a wide silver barrette on her head and into a twist, of a face that was drawn but for the live embarrassment there; because if she would not look at me, I would look; and as she shrank from me, I grew and filled the room. I knew my object and would not vary it or my route to it, however imperfect.

"Hope has been in the hospital," Josephina reported.

"I heard," I said. "What a thing."

"She's in good shape now," said Darren. "She had a rough go. We worried." And then to throw that sentiment aside, away, because they could now, at last, he added, "She had a little? What? . . . Sex sickness?"

"No," said Hope too quietly. "Don't."

"We have been teasing her," said Josephina, grabbing a pillow to insert behind Hope and so tempt the straight-edge of her into the couch. "Behaving like a teenager was what did this so we cannot resist."

Hope lowered her head, already tallying, I imagined, the cost of letting herself become so vulnerable.

"Good lord," Darren exhorted, "her daughter Danielle was at the hospital day and night for what? Four or five days? What a kid. Have you met her?" He eyed me.

"Oh, yes," I said.

"A beauty," he offered, waiting for me to elaborate or at least agree, and when I didn't, he went on with the thoughts running in his head. "But acting for all the world like her mother was already gone and carting in enormous bouquet after bouquet of these terrifying lilies that smelled like an ancient funeral parlor."

"She loves lilies," whispered Hope. "Not gardenias," she added, perhaps for me.

"She is a strong girl," said Josephina, her accent taking most of the sting out of her observations. "She sees tragedy for her everywhere. Life is more exciting like this. Can I get you a drink? We have emptied many bottles— she shouldn't drink—but water maybe, with bubbles?"

"No. I'm fine. I came to talk to Hope. Something has come up."

Darren fell into a wingchair—"Ah, news! Tell us! *Tell* us." Excited, he leaned forward and pulled something shiny from his pocket. "May I?" It looked like a lighter but wasn't, because he lay it flat in his palm, and brought it to his mouth.

"Don't fill the room with your herbs. She's been sick to death," scolded Josephina.

"This is prescribed for the sick, all kinds of sick."

"I don't care," said Hope, head still bent and her voice

so devoid of inflection that the words went up like a tired wall and then just fell over. She could have been addressing Darren, herself, or no one.

"I should probably speak to Hope alone," I said.

Darren lit his contraption, which prompted Josephina to open windows, huffing. "You are a selfish ass," she told him.

"And you're a beautiful piece of ass." In short order, he took a drag of what I understood was pot, again pot, and then blew a voluptuous plume of smoke above our heads. "And she's fine, right, Hope, darling? Doesn't she look fine? Shouldn't we celebrate? I'm happy to share." He turned to me. "My God, what a few days."

Hope pulled her robe up around her throat. "It's about Les," she said to them, nodding toward me.

Josephina sat down beside Hope and tossed her hands toward her friend. "*That* man. That *man*." She had such a talent for exasperation and went on, scoffing, "A fever so high as that." To me she said, "A urinary tract disturbance, she had, and did not address it? How?" She faced Hope, her voice almost gentle. "How does a woman not know? There are indications." To me, "We feel *everything,* no?"

"A free woman," Darren said, smoke coursing from his nose, "who couldn't leave the buffet. Who can blame her with all that she's been through? Where is he anyway, your Goliath?"

Hope leaned herself into Josephina, though her posture remained brittle. She leaned in to hide her face in her friend's neck as she said, sighing, "I expect he's just getting home from the hospital."

"What?" laughed Darren. "Did he pull his groin?"

"I should probably explain this part," I told them, and I did. I laid it out in a few short statements, spare of detail or editorializing or emotion, and as I did—*he wouldn't be reasoned with, wouldn't leave, so when I opened the door and he charged me, I hit him, with a golf club*—I grew more certain and more relaxed, and Hope more faraway, obscure. I had not been distracted by her or any of them, and I knew that this story, with every telling, meant my own story was safe. The story I would not tell. It signaled a victory of boundaries held at whatever the cost and in that propriety, my brand of it, yes, mine as told, broadcast, was the necessity that she, Hope, would have to leave.

She stood up abruptly but still did not look me in the eyes. "I have to rest now. I have to shower."

Darren was slow to move. "You'd rather break his head than let him break your door?"

I made them wait for my reply as I waited for Hope to look at me; when she did, I said to her: "I didn't think he would stop with my door."

"Well, brava, landlady. I tell you if there were any booze left in this place, I'd raise a glass to you."

"Get up, you idiot," Josephina said. "We have to let her alone."

"Time to go already?" he said, eyes and smile loose as yolk.

"We can come back anytime, give me a moment's notice and I am back," Josephina said, kissing Hope lightly on both cheeks. "Drink water. Sleep a lot."

Hope breathed a thank-you but did not hold anyone's eyes or take her hands from the base of her throat, where she still held her robe closed.

"Goodbye, baby." Darren gave her a loud kiss on her cheek. "Behave a little, huh? I'll come back in the morning."

"Call first," Hope told him.

They moved to the door but stopped short to wait for me. "Shall we go now?" said Josephina to me.

"In a minute. I have a matter I must discuss with Hope. . . . Alone."

They hovered until Hope gave her okay and pointed them to the door with her chin. "Go," she said.

"She needs her rest," Josephina reproved. She would hold her ground.

"She does. I know. I won't stay long."

"Go," said Hope again. "Go. I'm tired."

Josephina inched out while staring back at me; a barrage of black daggers from her black unmoving eyes.

The door shut, I looked at Hope and past her: "I'm sorry, Hope, it's awkward timing—" I began, just as I'd rehearsed, "but I think we both know—"

Her hands went up in front of her, chest high. "Wait! *Wait.* Please. I know this will sound crazy, but I'm not going to be able to do this without a shower. I have to . . . I need to be . . . *clean.*"

I paused, regarding her with her hands still up, her head to one side. She expected me to argue. I didn't have to. "I can wait," I said but did not move, would not.

"Here?" She cocked her head at me.

"Yes."

"Fine."

"Good."

She did not bother to shut the door completely, as if to prove to me she would not run. I heard the water go on with the robust pressure I'd intended for these apartments, for my tenants; steam would rise fast and reliably. I touched the books in their piles. I reshelved some. I put another pillow on the couch, folded an afghan over one of its arms. I was not her jailer. I was something else entirely. I paired the shoes that had mates and segregated those that didn't. Somehow I would teach her about order. For courage, I leafed through George's Simone de Beauvoir, an old Franklin hardcover edition of *The Second Sex,* trying to concentrate on the words, succeeding and failing, mostly failing. It was a long shower. In the kitchen, I washed several glasses and filled two with tap water for us. Then I sat as comfortably as I could to one side of the couch and breathed through any agitation, breathing the room, even the Lysol that went in sharp, taking the room back, even the building, the right to my sanity or my version of it. After we'd come to an understanding, I'd go back to my apartment and watch an old film; I'd give myself that. One watched with him. Yes. *His Girl Friday* with its snapping speeches or

Wings of Desire to see that girl swing from her trapeze, to watch an angel fall, willingly. I'd take *Lady into Fox* from its Ziploc bag, try to scent the day I shared it with him last.

"Sorry," she said, emerging. "I needed it to be," she searched for the word she wanted, "thorough."

Her wet hair had been combed away from her face and down her back in a dark channel, dampening the silk of her robe over her shoulders and in the space between them. She was makeup-less, making an exhibit of all the lines around her mouth and between and around her large gold-blue eyes, of the shadows under them, in the hollows of her cheeks, stealing over her upper lip. This was her show of starkness, but it didn't work, because in giving up on any defense and the tension that that required of her face, even of her carriage, she appeared tender. The lines that her face had earned looked impossibly yielding, and she smelled so fiercely of her—her perfume in the soap or shampoo she'd used, but also of something essentially her; yes, a high richness, as of good soil and sea salt. I sipped my water, suddenly realizing I'd let go the thread I'd held in my head for days. I waited too long searching for it so that she spoke before I could:

"Did you hit him hard?"

"No. Or, well, I did what I had to."

"He has a concussion, you know. But they've let him go."

"He's called you?"

"Exactly a hundred times."

"That many times?"

"A lot. Too much . . ."

"Did you give him keys?"

"Yes. No." She sat next to me on the couch. "He took a set and I didn't stop him."

I cleared my throat; I pushed through the static of all the questions I wanted to ask: Was he angry? Was he coming here? "He urinated in my elevator," I announced.

She checked my face to see if I was inventing this. I was, or in part. I'd nearly forgotten, and I didn't know who had done it. It was merely a test, of my nerve, hers.

She shrugged. "I don't know about that."

"But it's possible?"

"Yes, I suppose anything is. We got pretty high. Pretty out there."

I could see him in the act. The arrogance. The indifference. I breathed in, out. The horrid Lysol in the room. "I think we both know you have to go, I mean, to leave here."

She nodded, hands in her lap, face pointed there again.

I went on: "It's been a bad time, a hard time for you, no one blames you, I don't, but this place, my home, can't continue to be a stage for all you're doing to yourself."

She held herself in, barely seeming to breathe.

"I won't judge, or not beyond admitting I can understand everything you're going through enough that I can't live in proximity to it. Can you understand why . . ." I had to swallow. My voice had turned tiny, a whisper, like hers only moments ago. ". . . Why it is I must ask you to go?"

"I'll go. Of course."

We sat listening to each other's silence. We sat for several minutes.

I felt exhausted. I seized on the thread again and let it pull me: "I'll give you the time you need. Any help. I won't ask for money from you or George. Money is—has never been—the issue. It's . . ."

"*Separateness.* Respecting each other's *separateness.*"

She was quoting me, from the first day George had brought her to me. I did not know if she was mocking me, but the listlessness of her voice said otherwise.

"He called you Celie that day. You didn't like it, did you?"

I didn't answer. I was too amazed.

"I think you didn't like it."

She had taken notice of me that day. Creating intimacies where there were none, then; but now, now was something else entirely.

"Of course I have offended you, Celia, in your home, but do I have to tell you that I'm not like this, not usually? And that Les—I know it will sound incredible—but that Les is a good man?"

"You have nothing to apologize for. Not to me. And Les? I don't know him, and I don't need to."

She sniffed once, and I stole another look at her to see tears now. She let them fall into her lap and sink into the fabric of the silk.

"A tissue? Can I—"

"I'll be okay. I'm all right."

Was she quoting me again?

"Yes," I said. "Yes." She would make me cry. I did not want that. "You have good friends. Lovely children. Leo—"

"He is a miracle, my son. My daughter, too, but he's always been so complete, so completely himself—"

"Yes."

"That's why it's all so shaming, that it hurts this much, that I can't seem to put what's happened in my marriage in any perspective. Being replaced. It's all so wretchedly common, and I have so very much to be grateful for. I guess that makes it a little worse. I can't help it. I love my husband, our family as it was, and so it's as though a part of me is gone, as though I have a hole here, where he was, we were, that everyone can see." She placed her fist into her diaphragm. "Here." She drew a circle around it, hit it once lightly, laughing an empty laugh. "Bull's-eye," she said, and then hit the spot harder still and so on with every "here, here, here," escalating, the laughter giving way to protest and more tears, coming faster.

"Please," I said. "I can't," and I stood and lurched for the door and my apartment and the movies I'd watch alone and a book that might still smell of the simple homeliness of bean soup and a time that had made perfect sense once.

But I did not get far. I turned back, knelt down, and took her fist in my hand, unfisted it, elongating finger by finger. "Stop. Stop now. I know about this, and I know this won't help." My hand went to her forehead, a fever maybe, however slight. "You're not well, please," I said into her weeping as it turned to moaning, her robe soaked in widening spots. She could not catch her breath. Her mouth wide open with sound. She jerked her hand away and collapsed onto her side, curling herself up, all of her into another fist. Both hands jammed between her legs and jerking into her with the complaint: "I wake up and realize, he's *even here, here* where he is! I want him out of me!"

I slid in behind her on the couch and wrapped myself around her, endeavoring to still her. I stayed her hands by holding my hand to them, pressing them into her. She let me as she moved through the heaving she'd given herself to and couldn't stop easily and then slipped her hands out so my hand was alone between her legs, over the silk of the robe and nothing else. "Les. Call Les," she pleaded and, before I could take my hand away, she squeezed my hand between her legs, with her thighs, doing her pleading with them. "I need him."

"No, no," I breathed into her ear.

"It hurts. It won't stop."

I arranged myself like a vise around her, to remind her what it was to be contained—her upset, her desire, her choices, the bad ones too. Her salt in my mouth, I started to tell her about the Maine sea roses, *rugosa,* and how they grew like weeds, despite the elements, despite adversity; but she could not hear me over her complaints, the regular pleas and now the struggling, the struggling against me, to get away from me, to the phone. But I was a tourniquet, however poor, against the woundedness dissolving her into liquid that kept flowing into me. What had Melville said? She would keep me from remembering myself. . . . *A deadly drain,* yes . . . *Yet so vast is the quantity of blood . . . and so distant and numerous its interior fountains, that the animal will keep thus bleeding and bleeding for a considerable period; even as in a drought a river will flow.* . . . I had to bring her here, with me, I had to be ingenious enough to shut her up.

With my free hand I reached for the fleece of her earlobe; then I touched her breast, I touched her in all the places I knew to touch, places where her husband must have touched her with love once—her husband who touched someone else now. I made her feel the pressure of my palm and the strength of my arm—that not everything was lost, was draining from her, that she could be held, could be whole as she arched into me now wedged behind her on the couch. I had never touched breasts but my own, never felt a cunt, never known the incredible softness of a woman not just in these places but in her skin up and down the length of her long light bones pushing into me. I told her she was beautiful over and over. I became my husband and so became more of me and reminded her of tenderness's returns; as she wept, I kept reminding her with my hand, cupping, tracing, and fingering her, to show her every expression of the extraordinary softness that was still there, still her. He hadn't taken it or the grace of her long light bones. I reminded her that she'd been a woman loved and would be again and could be now, here, as my mouth found the nerves on the back of her neck, licking at the traces of her perfume, the stubborn sweet and savory of it, her sweat, her tears running from her eyes to my mouth. I did not say "my beautiful" but just *beautiful, beautiful* as I continued to tell her flesh of its gifts, such pleasure, gently but insistently given, even biting her earlobe with my front teeth, sweeping her hair from her face, her neck, as she cried and breathed less jaggedly, "It hurts, it hurts." I did not stop until it stopped hurting, until I heard pleasure articulated from her. Her throat as open as her body, wet everywhere from tears and the coming, and I did hear it, a long high twisting cry and a twisting in my arms as my fingers dove up and up into the full expressive wetness of her. *Hold me, hold me. Here and here,* she said after she came, placing one of my hands between her legs to press again, another over her breasts. *Hold me tight.*

SHAPE-SHIFTING

———

I WATCHED HER SLEEP. I watched her wake and reach for me as if she were a child and I reached back and took her warm hand in both of mine as she went under again, her body tensing and going slack with her dreams and, I supposed, with deciding to return to the day and me, and twice at least, choosing not to, turning away, back into sleep.

I did not begrudge her it. I slipped out of the apartment before she could ask me to go, but I came back with a book or two, one in particular that had balanced me and my husband, a prized something to share if asked to; and I came back with my watchfulness.

I couldn't complicate matters, or further complicate them, from a lack of resolve, so I waited until she decided to wake, as she finally did, and to look blinking at me as if I were made of dust that had gotten in her eyes. She sat up, pulling her head up last, the afghan I'd laid over her shrugged off and exposing her breasts. She searched for and then covered herself with the silk robe that had become balled up under her. There was no panic in her gestures, but still I stood up to give her room to decide how our story would go now. I shook all expression from my face. It was not easy because I'd already admitted, and allowed to travel all through me, in an instant, less, the electric joy of her in my arms, having transformed her and so having been transformed, knowing something of what my husband felt when he'd made love to me and then things I had never known and might never again. Yes, I admitted to having loved her as I took her skin on the couch, and in less than an instant also allowed there'd be no more, that she'd turn away from me again, backwards to Les or something or someone else or forward, out the door and gone, just as I'd requested.

I sat on the wingchair that wasn't George's, stiffly, telling myself I could take it all with me. I was a collector, a conjurer, had been since I'd become a widow. I'd had practice—in this way I told myself I was protected.

"I'm so hungry," she said dreamily, after she'd tied her robe to cover her and the soft nearly transparent hairs of her torso and neck, the brown upturned nipples on breasts that had known the sun, that pointed slightly to either side of her, yes, that hung but were dense and full in the hand, not flaccid, not empty, bigger than my own, and more generous in every way, unshy of how they'd been used and would yet be.

"I'd like to cook us something. It always makes me feel at home——" She interrupted herself to look at me, to consider me there. I heard myself swallow and held my breath because I wasn't certain whether she had determined what to make of me and my hands and even my mouth on her, how I had insisted on all of it, despite my speeches. I was prepared to explain why there was no reason to be ashamed, to tell her things I'd never told anyone so she could better fathom it and maybe me, when she suddenly smiled at me. No, it was more: she shined at me, from her cheeks and eyes and the wide shape of her open mouth, and then laughed at me. "Why are you way over there?"

I had a rash of replies, full laughter of my own, but I wouldn't open my mouth to any of it.

"Sit beside me," she said, gentle flirting in her voice.

I did, but she did not touch me and I did not touch her.

"I haven't been able to shop. Maybe we could order some food in?" she ventured.

"Sure."

"And I have a prescription to fill."

"I can go get it."

"I can call someone."

"I'd be glad to go."

"I'll order something to eat for delivery. It will be here waiting for you when you get back."

I dove into a day outside the building that was gray but roughed open with wind and fat clouds tumbling to out-pace the sun. I hurried and stalled, set off again, arriving at her pharmacy on Court Street, doing what I'd come for, as a friend or a nurse or a neighbor might, nothing beyond the ordinary after all, and back into the wind of a day I could not remember encountering as I was encountering this one, dragging sensation over me, loosening my face, the muscles of my legs. I did not know what we would say to one another when I returned, and when I imagined our conversation I became embarrassed from what was in turns excitement and dread, but I went back more eagerly than I'd done anything in years.

"My husband used to like to be read to, when he was ill," I told her as I passed back into her, the door of the apartment shut and locked behind us.

"No one has read to me in a long time."

She'd laid out a city of cartons on the coffee table—Indian, Chinese, Italian. "I didn't know what you liked," she said, finding her smile for me again. "I went for everything."

"Oh, it's all lovely."

And it was. How rare it was for any one of us—to be found, without warning, freed from the rigors of disap-proving of someone, of wanting to, and for your desire to please to be met in equal measure, with the same readiness. I didn't know how long it would last, but while it did, it was like what I imagined singing well with someone was like or walking with someone, with the same length of step and rhythm of stride.

I took up one of the plates there and served myself as large a helping as the plate would allow as she talked of food—how Louis XIV had at least four hundred cooks working to make his meals and how in New York we have the same, more, thousands of restaurants, dozens of cuisines at our disposal. How do we decide? Good oils, the quality of the meat or proximity, price, impulse? "You walk down a block in this town and suddenly you've spent twenty dollars and filled your stomach with something you had no idea you were hungry for. . . ." She talked for both of us with her voice alert and soothing—she talked, in fact, about wonder. I ate and watched her pick and chew while she chatted on, about suckling pig in Chinatown and then truffles to be had here—I remembered something about truffles from her journal, yes, truffle oil she'd described like heaven poured into her, and then, as if someone had passed a cold hand over her, she faded, her energy gone, like that. "Whoa," she said. "All of a sudden . . ." She sat back. "I'm wrung out."

I took the antibiotics from the bag, refilled her water glass.

"Take this." She held one hand under mine as she took the pill from my palm. "Do you want to lie down?" I readied a throw to cover her with.

"In the bedroom," she said, "not on this couch again."

"You should rest now." I would go if that was what she needed. I could teach myself to be satisfied with what had happened. A surprise still.

She let out a sigh. "Would you—"

Would you mind leaving was what I heard already, was prepared for. Yes, I was ready to do whatever she most needed.

"Would you come with me?" is what she said instead.

"In there?" I asked.

She laughed. "Lie down with me."

On clean sheets, we talked of the hospital, the noise and the nurses, and of our George and agreed we missed him. The room had been tidied, the windows left cracked so that we could hear the wind speed and whistle outside, but neither of us got up to let more of it in. We lay side by side, an inch or two between us, but I did not touch her, or she me; we were close enough to know the heat the other generated and in this way we were joined and it was enough. The book I'd brought up from my apartment, *Lady into Fox,* freed from its seal, still did smell faintly of soup. I told her the book was a fairy tale for adults, about a marriage and miracles, though not the sort that delivers you necessarily or solves any human concern, that it was originally published in 1922, and that it wasn't long. I did not tell her why I'd kept the book sealed away; it was enough that I'd preserved it and that I had it here with her.

There may not be one marvel to speak of in a century, and then often enough comes a plentiful crop of them; monsters of all sorts swarm suddenly upon the earth, comets blaze in the sky, eclipses frighten nature, meteors fall in rain . . .

"I like it," she whispered.

"You can fall asleep."

"I can't."

"Why?"

"I'm too exhausted." With her pinkie finger, she hooked a strand of my hair away from my face. "I'm too excited. No one's read to me in years."

. . . But the strange event which I shall here relate came alone, unsupported, without companions into a hostile world, and for that very reason claimed little of the general attention of mankind. For the sudden changing of Mrs. Tebrick into a vixen is an established fact which we may attempt to account for as we will. . . .

The sprouting of a tail, the gradual extension of hair all over the body, the slow change of the whole anatomy by the process of growth, though it would have been monstrous, would not have been so difficult to reconcile to our ordinary conceptions, particularly had it happened in a young child.

But here we have something very different. A grown lady is changed straightaway into a fox. There is no explaining that away by natural philosophy. The materialism of our age will not help us here.

"Is this a happy or sad story?" Hope asked me.

"Maybe melancholy. About the way things go. We anticipate one story and we get another."

"Is the woman cursed?"

"No, that's just it. When the couple is walking along in the woods, they hear a fox hunt in the distance and then suddenly she changes. There's no clear reason and the author doesn't ever really provide one."

Hope nodded: "Well, fantastic or not, life is like that, isn't it? We are all shape-shifting, whether we want to or not. It's shocking; you blink and . . ."

I went on with my reading, yes, through outward change of a woman into fox, through Mrs. Tebrick nonetheless dressing in her elegant gowns and eating at table much as the lady she believes she yet is, will be again, through the gradual inward change, as she becomes a fox entirely, when she begins to feel caged by their house and their walled garden, and even bites her husband when he assays to correct her behavior and remind her of who she was, of her propriety, what he took to be her humanity.

"You were married?" Hope asked me, a finger briefly on my wedding band.

"I was."

"He passed?"

"He did."

"So young."

"Yes."

"What was it?"

"That killed him?"

"Yes."

"Cancer. Caught too late."

"I wish mine were dead," she said.

"Do you?"

"Maybe, yes . . . no . . . Sometimes definitely."

"Tell me about him, if you'd like," I said.

"Oh, god. There's too much. Tell me about yours first."

"I can't."

"Why?" she asked, rolling on her side and dropping a hand lightly on my hip.

But I'd already gripped the book to me, and my body had gripped its bones. I closed my eyes to tell her the truth, as I'd understood it all these years: "Because he's all mine."

She rolled away from me then. She was quiet a long time. She'd wanted to barter, that's what was expected, made for confidences, but she didn't know how practiced I was, and how careful, at preserving him, just as we'd agreed, his voice reading *Moby-Dick,* his hips moving in a slow circle, as he danced into me, making love, the gold in his skin all year but especially when the days grew longer, how warm it became suddenly all over him, as if he were blooming too, from the inside out, and when I could feel my heart shifting into the endless expanse of him, as it did, she said: "And my cheating, lying husband is all mine, my life, my history, and then in a blink, not mine at all anymore. Not now."

"You don't have to talk about it if you don't—"

But she couldn't stop herself, for the wonder of it all again, how relentlessly monotonous a long marriage could be, no matter how comforting, how respectful, and then something, a smell, a song, the color in a late-day sky could bring them back to each other, the why of their days. Or a suit in the closet. *How crisp he always looked in suits,* she said. *And this one blue suit, the one he walked home in on 9/11, covered in dust. Many of his colleagues and friends gone while he walked back to our life, the house in Cobble Hill, the children, in that suit. He asked me to throw it away, but I wouldn't. I got it cleaned. I restored it. How many times can something be restored? As many times as you're willing to do the work, right? Or that's what I thought. . . . But maybe that's when I lost him, when I put my bid on how things can survive, how we could, when what he wanted was to forget and let go and know new things, a new woman.*

With some violence she shook her head as if to be free of a gnat assailing her and rolled over abruptly to straddle me. She, taller than I, older and more beautiful. Was she making all the same calculations I was? That she'd been able to live more, risk more, and for what? Me? Here, now? She ran a fingertip over the planes of my face—my forehead, my cheekbones—as if drawing it into something she understood and then moved her hand heavily between my breasts down to the rise of my belly to where my pants were resolutely fastened, stopping there. "Can I kiss you?" she asked, and I consented with a nod, though I wasn't sure I should have or wanted to. But there was a wife in a story I'd just read, one whose husband ultimately loved her more as a fox than he had when she was a woman—I'd not had a chance to read that part to Hope yet—that Mr. Tebrick devoted himself to her in ways he hadn't ever imagined when she became something other than the woman he'd married, than the woman the wife had planned on being, and there was that blue suit left in the closet, more men's clothes abandoned or waiting or perhaps gone now, a ghost already in Hope's house, and so she gave me her lips, at first tentative and formal, exploring, then looser, fitting her lips above, between, and over mine, then hungry, then lushly wet and unconscious. A woman who became a fox like that. No explanation. And Hope and I, stranded with one another, orphans remaking our world.

She fell back into the bed after having answered her phone at last. It had been going off at intervals throughout the afternoon into evening. I supposed she'd listened to her messages, too, and now, her eyes on the ceiling, her hair loose and swallowing us, she said, "I'll go."

"Let's not talk about it now," I said because of her hair, because it was so soft and extravagant between us.

"But I have conditions."

"What sort?"

"Come to my house."

"That's the first?"

"Yes."

"And?"

"A party. With all your tenants. And some of my friends. A going-away party."

"You don't have to go anywhere."

"George will be back soon enough, and I should be with my kids. I should try to remember myself."

I had nothing to say to this. I could not advocate against what she thought best for her. What I had advocated for.

"So my tenants and your Darren?"

"I'll cook."

"A big mess of a meal." Now I was quoting her.

"The same."

YOUTH IS WILLINGNESS

——

YOUTH IS WILLINGNESS. Les had said that to achieve an end the night of George's going-away party so many weeks ago now, but perhaps he knew that willingness also meant such tickling strangeness, staying a course, on the thinness of a high wire, when every bit of good sense is telling you to find stable ground.

She'd made sure to let me go with marching orders last night—indeed with order set against the confusion of our intimacy. I agreed to her conditions, to plans. A kindness; how generous she was with her affections when her most long-held ones had been so affronted.

And I was more youthful than I'd been in years and famished, and every time I heard her move upstairs I blushed or laughed out loud or ran to tunnel into my bed—I could not stop eating the leftovers she'd packed me off with and I sipped whiskey to calm myself; I was careful only to sip; I could not lose my head and reduce this solitude that I was collapsing into gratefully to a prison or a rejection. I had more than a meal with her, one I'd not foreseen, and my delight flooded through me and filled the empty spaces of my apartment and climbed the walls to her feet and higher, the whole building hugged into me, into my delight. I had discovered I had a sort of life here—one I'd planned and not. There was the horror of not being able to affect one's plans in life, but then there was the relief at times of being released from them, from a world you predicted, mastered too well.

I had never been with a woman, and though she didn't say, she hadn't either or not recently enough for her to draw on. But I supposed there are things all adults come to know about the body, male or female, or want to know; and once appetite has been admitted to once, asked and answered for between two people (along with its parade of sensations), summoning appetite again isn't hard. I gave her what I knew to give, again, what had been given me, and it was a revelation. But when she tried to answer in kind, her hands became shy. She could not work the buttons of my shirt or the front latch of my bra without her fingers getting in the way. Impatient, she shoved my shirt and bra up to my neck like a teenage boy might. She needed force to overcome and discount the awkwardness, to recall a part in a performance with which she was familiar. (What had someone said at George's party? It's all performance; it depends if one believes in the delivery.) At the sight of my breasts, she started, mine so unlike hers, smaller, paler, a girl's rose nipples, and it was what they told her of my age rather than of my sex that stopped her and broke whatever spell she'd wanted to generate. She bent to examine them more closely and then cupped them as if they were each as soft and vulnerable as the head of an infant, as if they were too precious, and then she became dazed. Another woman. Away and into another woman. A younger woman.

I took her hands in each of mine. The meal between us had been affection and that's all I'd intended as it was happening, or hoped for.

"You're like a girl, your body," she said, "and yet you seem so old, but you're not really, are you? How old are you?"

She'd bumped into the strangeness of it, of me, the young widow, and what we had done, just as the day only yesterday gave up outside the windows and began to retract its expanse. The windowpanes already foreshortening the room and reflecting the bedroom back at us.

Her cell phone had been humming and beeping in the other room, and every time she did not answer it, did not notice it, I had become more confident of my own hands, that I didn't need to see her face to know it, with us arranged on our sides with her back against the front of me, as before. Yes, we'd been in step and it didn't occur to us to question it. But when her cell rang once more, she turned her head to it. I pushed my bra back down, rearranged my shirt.

She sighed a laugh that wasn't really a laugh at all: "You know my son has a crush on you."

"I have a crush," I said but wasn't sure she'd heard, "on both of you."

"That's probably my daughter."

"You should probably answer—"

She interrupted with "Is it hot in here?" and was up to open the windows wider so that night came in the room and the wind; then her phone, which had gone mum, started again.

I daydreamed extravagantly; my recall went off in unpredictable bursts. And between errands I ran in Brooklyn, April in Brooklyn, to the grocery, to Macy's for new linens and down pillows (why not?), to the liquor store for bottles of red wine from exotic places, a girl's face came to me—I'd not reassembled it in years. The slight overbite, the deep brown of her small thickly lashed eyes, the straight hang of her dirty blond hair. Daphne Rogers. She and I had had an addicting complicity that could only end in heartbreak for one or both of us—but for over a year we passed clothes and magazines and secrets between us; we saw one another or talked by phone every day, used the same cloyingly scented shampoos, Finesse or Suave, the same neon nail polish, and powdery deodorants, and were still young enough that we slept in the same bed, encircling each other with limbs and promises of all we'd do together, things no one had ever done, creating symmetry in every way we could against the disorder of being teenagers. We did not regard each other sexually, or not as sexual destinations or opportunities, but as partners in the adventure of adolescence, of becoming female in a way that thrilled and terrified us but did not yet shame us. She was darker, her breasts already fuller, waist longer, her thumbs curved back in a way mine could not. I thought her prettier and she was quick to say the same of me, and during the second summer of our friendship we lay on the beach for hours, sacrificing every teenaged bit of us to the sun, and one afternoon when we'd both turned improbably brown, though she browner, always, we held hands as we fell asleep and woke after sunset, when the world over that truncated Long Island Sound beach had turned vast and pink and a purple-stained gray; and we laughed and laughed, crying and falling off our bikes from laughing, never-minding shoes or cover-ups, as we bolted from Weed Beach to get to my house for dinner, to my mother who scolded less, who let us sip white wine, Sancerre or Chardonnay, from my father's shot glasses.

It was me who was left for a boy. That separation had instructed me on loneliness but also on the pleasures of longing. Daphne held on to that unremarkable boy through high school, off and on through college. She insisted on marrying him at twenty-three, even though she and Paul had nothing in common save endurance and a first love that had become, it seemed to me, something of a sentence. Daphne appeared determined to become unremarkable with Paul in every way. She still lives in our hometown or she did last I heard. But for a long time, through my teens, and especially when I made a new friend, she was all I thought I needed to feel whole again.

I could hear everything Hope did above me—my hearing her interrupted me mid-cleaning or eating or trying to wash or sleep. I heard her singing through my open window. I heard her vacuuming. I heard the race of her shower water shoosh through the plumbing in the walls, the toilet flush. I gathered up some movies I'd longed to watch, missed like you missed old friends, from my storage space—*My Brilliant Career, Notorious, Wings of Desire,* and *His Girl Friday.* I entertained inviting her down to encounter some of Cary Grant's exquisite face, but my apartment's spareness might translate to her in ways that would be distracting, and I heard her friends and family coming and going, laughter, and her doorbell, which had the same stuttering high bell as my own, trilled through the walls. She came down to my door three times in three days. She'd baked zucchini bread "to keep busy" and late morning wanted me to have a loaf "while it was still warm." The next day, after I'd returned from the grocery, she needed to borrow soap for the dishwasher. And then, on the last visit, she came to set a day for us to go to her home or "what was my home," she said, trailing off. "Can you still come?" Yes, of course, day after tomorrow, certainly, see you then, but I would not stand outside her door and knock; I would not telephone. I had seen the look on her face when she was confronted with me beneath her. To pursue her in any way risked pressing on that foreignness again. I had to know better by now.

Last night she tapped on the floor of her bedroom, over my own, or I think she did. A one-two-three, pause, and another one-two-three. Was I inventing it, half-asleep? With a broom handle I tapped back. Yes, I was here. I was there.

THE HIGH WIRE

———

THE DIALOGUE IN MOST FILMS, I had read, runs at a speed of roughly 100 to 140 words a minute. *His Girl Friday* runs at upwards of 240—it's a herky-jerky race toward the finish at which a man and a woman marry or at least pledge to, once again, in this case a divorced couple taking another shot at union. But the speed, the inside jokes making reference to Cary Grant's real name—Archie Leach—and the uninviting look at small-town domestic life, and even at its opposite—a professional life as newspaper reporters in the city filthy with egos, runarounds, corruption, and, again, such haste to get the story, meet the paper's deadline—signal that the film is first and foremost about the absurdity of valuing any role above another or even believing in

them, or not for long. What Hildy the woman reporter—
played by Rosalind Russell for all the part's grit and myriad
frustration and strength—or Walter, played by Cary Grant,
can choose is speed and excitement, outrunning thinking
about anything for too long. They choose the high-stakes,
excessively caffeinated (if not by coffee then by competition)
world of the human city with its often inhuman demands;
so much like the world New York lived in now, post-9/11,
streaming with the need to survive, and one, since I was
widowed, I had long felt reaching for me everywhere,
waiting at the building's entrance, and one I had resisted,
opted out of. But now with the film in my DVD player, the
fast cuts, the speeches, one overlapping with another, I
kept up. I had a glass of wine and a slice of store-bought
quiche, the sort (apart from the store-boughtness) I was
sure Hope would approve of, and I trapped every word,
trying hard not to listen to the movements above and
around me and what their speed or lack of it might mean
for seeing Hope tomorrow, when we'd go to her home, or
what was her home, on an errand that was still not clear to
me because, the truth was, I didn't care what it entailed.

I turned up the film's volume once, twice, while the
wine softened my nerves, but despite all this, I heard him
at her door.

Or *felt* him—maybe when you nearly kill someone or
wish to, you are joined in ways that one cannot name or
know.

I heard the bell upstairs go once. Then nothing. I lowered the film's sound to make out a determined but controlled rapping at her door, but the door would not open so the bell was sounded again, a long report traveling the walls to me. Then his voice calling, calling to her in a way I recognized. Words which might have been *C'mon, we can't live like this* to nothing but a door between them. Did he use his key or did she buzz him in through the building's entrance? Did she mistake him for someone else? Or was she playing at something?

Odds were if she kept the door closed, he'd come to me next. There were certain scripts that we all keep playing at, and I understood Les's character that well—that someone had to be accountable when events did not go his way. What I took to be Hope's lightly insistent one-two-three came over my head and then again. Was I imagining it?

Either way, I turned off the DVD and went directly to my phone, scanned the numbers on the call history until I found Brazo's. "The man who tried to assault me is back in the building," I said to his voice mail. "I do not know who let him in or why. Can you call or come, yes, maybe that? Can you come?"

I found the broom and tapped back to Hope. *I'm here. I'm there.*

She called back to him, reasoning, perhaps trying to be gentle. I opened my own apartment door so that I could decipher it all better. If I heard any violence in him or his hands, I'd race there, but I did not. He said please. *Please, baby. I just want to see you for a minute. Please. What is all this?*

He waited. In silence. So did Hope. So did I.

She'd read to me before I left her. She chose an American novel set in France. It starts by describing an American man taking a train into the French countryside, away from Paris, descending into color, alongside shocks of hay and trees and village roads and their intimacies bending away and out of sight. "Les offered to take me to Autun," she said to me beside her, yet in her bed. "But I think he'd be uncomfortable. He doesn't like France. It's too small. I mean physically mostly; he thinks it's a country of no consequence really—everything for him is about conquest. He can't help it; he'd sneer at it. Isn't that awful?" And because we wanted a laugh, we envisioned how one would go about domesticating Les, how we'd tie and collar him and order him about. Put him on his knees. "Sex as a prize for good behavior" for a man like Les, who she said could dazzle a woman's body by doing so little, just a word, a tone of voice. She said, "My god, the delicious strength of men," and then she thought about it, "if they know how to use it."

A rustling of paper of some sort on her landing upstairs. A sniff and a hot breath let go. I could hear even his heartbeat, I could feel him sweat, and with his hard-soled shoes once more tapping over my floors and trouser fabric swishing, all broadcasting his intentions, he took off down the stairs.

Quickly closing my apartment door, I flipped the DVD

back on, and tossed into my seat. A gulp of wine. A prayer. I crossed legs and arms, hugging myself. Let me be wrong. Let him just go. Go away.

C'mon, baby.

He treated my door with the formality he reserved for strangers. Knuckles only glancing the surface . . . One-two. How foolish I'd been to put the movie back on in a show of what? Normalcy or nonchalance? Another barrier between us, of sound? For he could hear it as well as I could. Where was the golf club? They'd returned it to me when it appeared no charges would be filed. This time, I assured myself, I could strike harder and keep on hitting. There was a history of recorded facts to draw from, a script, predictable, at least until you were inside it, playing it out.

Again the hard back of his hand in a one-two that was there and gone. No escalation expressed in the speed or force applied. I took the chance I could forestall it if I responded just then, "Yes?" through the door.

"It's Les," he said matter-of-factly, as if we were equal parts in a conspiracy, as if I didn't need more.

"Yes?"

"It's Les."

He sighed and paper or plastic fluttered on the other side of the door.

"I can't seem to get any women to open up today," he said to himself for my benefit. He regrouped: "Hey, look, I came to apologize."

"Big of you."

"What?"

I did not repeat myself.

"Is that the TV?"

Nothing from me.

"I acted . . . I was blotto, you know? I can't remember, but I know it was crazy. I was . . ." His voice arched
up in query. ". . . An ass, right?"

I held my breath for as long as I could.

"Yeah, well," he laughed, but tension began to file in
behind his words, "I have an egg on my head that leads me
to think you might have something to say to me."

"You're lucky to be alive," I told him loud enough to be
heard.

"Yeah," his voice still louder, the run of laughter this
time for show, "well, shit, aren't we all, lady?"

I didn't respond.

"I have flowers here. Two bouquets and from the looks
of it, no takers."

I squinted a look through the eyehole. He had one arm
extended, a giant hand I could not see resting against the
door, his great head hanging down, and enormous tumid
apricot roses punctuated by irises grew from his other side.

"I didn't press charges," he said. "I wouldn't."

"I didn't either," I said.

We breathed at each other through the door. His was
loose and even.

I opened the door before I could reconsider and startled him so his handsomeness had to resettle on his face.

He wore a light gray suit, expensive. His handsomeness shocked me still—his every line spoke of its privileges, that he could be hard or soft and life wouldn't penalize him. And his height lent him force even when he wasn't asserting it, even sober and contrite or trying contrite on. He'd shaved—his jaw was no less an object of masculinity, as inflexible as ice, but today the skin that dressed it was unexpectedly smooth and taut and unmarked as a young man's. Today, as he bid for composure, his free hand unmoored and flying awkwardly, straightening his tie, then hiding in his pant pocket, I saw something of a boy in his manner. Bashful, maybe nervous. Surely it had always been there and he worked against it, to be what was expected, a man of business, who dictated to the world, to women.

He talked of the flowers, that he'd visited the best florist in the city, on Fifth Avenue, at the end, near Washington Square. Did I know it? Still, he wasn't sure if they'd do the trick. He never was one for flowers though he'd bought them often enough. He spoke as if we were friends now that I'd opened my door and stood before him. He was good on the high wire and went on with relief, unused to being on the losing side of things, and gaining in assurance, knowing that if he aimed his mood high, I or anyone listening might be taken up there with him, with his charm.

"What are you watching in there?" And somehow he and his delicious strength were in my living room looking at my old TV and the barrenness I'd chosen to outfit the room in. "No frills, eh?" he said. "I get that. I can see it."

Why didn't I throw him out? Because I'd bested him before, because she was safer with him here than anyplace else, and because, most surprisingly of all, I wasn't afraid of him, and I liked it.

"What are you watching?"

I told him. He asked what I was drinking. I held up the wine bottle. "Have anything stronger?"

I went for the Jameson and two short glasses. When I came back, he'd already situated the only other chair in the room next to my own. He'd seated himself and abandoned the flowers on the credenza.

"This is a funny film."

"It is."

I poured for him.

He sipped, then gulped, and, his head thrown back, his enormous Adam's apple danced. He set about trying to acquaint his long trunk with the austerity of the high-backed chair, a dining room chair from a set I'd stored away.

"It's a little annoying, too."

"The film?"

"I mean, look at them go," he said.

"They don't quit or can't. That's the idea."

I turned up the volume as Hildy hollered, *Do you hear*

that? That's the story I just wrote. Yes, yes, I know we had a bargain. I just said I'd write it. I didn't say I wouldn't tear it up—

His body in the too small chair tensed. All of him coiling around an idea, real or imagined. She didn't let him in. I didn't either, at first, and now there was a mere hand's length between us.

—It's all in little pieces now, Walter, and I hope to do the same for you someday. And that, my friends, is my farewell to the newspaper game. I'm gonna be a woman, not a news-getting machine. I'm gonna have babies and take care of them. Give 'em cod liver oil and watch their teeth grow—

How long would it take Brazo to pick up my message? And would he come? Yes, odds were . . . The script. He would not fail to play the part assigned him; it would say too much about Brazo as a man.

"Does it have to be that loud?" he asked.

I didn't turn it down.

He gulped again, emptied the glass, and hunching over his knees, elbows posted on his thighs, he rolled the whiskey glass between his palms, back and forth, picking up speed.

Only one dull lamp lit the room. It gave off as much dimness as clarity and had no effect on the shadows pooling in the room's corners, at its edges. The screen jumped at us. I wrapped the hand farthest from him, my left, around the neck of the whiskey bottle, which I'd positioned between my legs. I was prepared to lift the bottle in an instant.

They took him to the county hospital, where they're awfully worried he'll recover.

Now Les simply held his glass in one hand and regarded it, as if it just spoke out of turn and he was deciding whether he should pitch it.

"I love her and I fucked it up," he announced. Arm outstretched, he extended his empty glass to me with his eyes on the room's shadows or farther out still, on the progress of his confession.

I poured for him and then myself.

"I let her use me."

I turned down the movie's volume then, though the images still raced at us. He drank. I drank.

"I thought I was in charge, but I wasn't. And I'm not now."

"She's not herself." I'd said this before, to whom? Leo? "What I mean is she doesn't know what that is."

He shook his head. "We went too far." He extended his arm to me again, and I poured again.

"Why no furniture?" he asked.

"More to clean." And as I drank down my portion of whiskey, needing to keep pace, I thought *more to ruin, to replace, to worry over.*

"Are you gay?"

"No." I wanted to editorialize but didn't, only added, "I was married . . . To a man."

"So you like men?"

"Some."

He finished his share again, shivered like a big horse, and then turned to trap me in his gaze for a moment, so unblinking and sure of itself, it burned. "But you love her, too?"

I didn't answer, though I saw what he was after—aligning the two of us, me with him, outside her, looking in with longing.

"We were kids together," he said. "She told you that, right? That we go way back?"

I nodded.

He closed his eyes, and my far hand gripped the bottle again, upside down, thumb extended to support my lifting it if I had to, as he recited: "I know the backs of her knees. I know the shape of her elbows. She used to eat tomatoes off the vine. She stole them in season and bit into them like apples. She climbed trees like us boys. She wore the same yellow bathing suit for years. A one-piece. She wouldn't give it up. . . . Her father was in insurance, worked hard enough to get by, but he was a bohemian type at heart. Her mother was gorgeous, tall. Like her . . . She can draw, you know, pictures, and she sings. Have you heard that?"

I shook my head. I wouldn't tell him what I knew and did not; he meant to drag me back to the strangeness, convince me that I didn't know her, couldn't, not like he did. He meant to best me at last.

"Hymns. She sang in church."

He could be lying. Who could say?

"I loved her then. I've loved her as long as I can remember. I planned on marrying her."

In a theatrical gesture of a man confiding, he laid his mitt of a hand over mine, my right, nearest him. He hoped for sympathy, to disarm me with it. I took my hand away.

After a showy sigh of disappointment, he punished me: "She told me you went into her place when she wasn't home."

"Landladies do that sometimes."

"Not without notification."

"I thought I smelled something. Gas. It was a precaution."

He laughed without looking at me. "Bullshit."

He was instructing me on my trespasses; I was no better than him, no different. I drank again. I'd already had too much.

"You drink like a man."

His hand on mine again. I closed my eyes and fought back, imagined collaring him—an unforgiving strap of leather around his neck, a rusty leash. Or chains. Yes, better. Hope and I had talked about him and turned him into a joke, hadn't we? Should I tell him? She didn't love him any more than she did me; we were necessary distractions, a jigsaw she was arranging like a hobbyist.

I let her use me, he'd said. Yes, a man who could be led. I'd not known the varying possibilities of a man's strength or lack of it in so terribly long. Hope hadn't been able to bridge the distance necessary to get to me on the other side, to put her hands on me with any real ease, but maybe she could cause him to. Hope could. He was desperate to please her now. He would be her body, her intention. This is how we would domesticate him at last. The long man between my legs, doing what he was told.

My head fell back into my chair. My hips moved, up, down. I'd lost them to the reverie. His hand rose and smothered my breast.

"So you said you like men?"

His hand was so big—the physical presence of him expanded—how did one not shrink when confronted with it? His palm pressed in, then eased up to press and circle again, a rhythm. I had to be in charge or else disappear into his voracity, but I did not speak as he lifted the bottle posted between my legs—"What were you going to do? Hit me with this?"—and pulled me toward him and onto his lap.

"Yeah, that's right, come here. . . . Shit," excitement on his breath on my face, "how old are you anyway?" Something was taking place that I dreaded as much as I seemed to need. A sickness muddled in and around the words ranging all through me, *fuck* and then *fuck me, fuck me;* how the words communicated NOW and don't stop and every other expression of obliterating time and me, me with it . . . But then a knock on the door. Polite. I almost did not believe in it. And then it came again—remarkable for its care. Hope saving me from something I might not come back from or not wholly. Or Brazo. Yes. At last.

"Ignore it," Les said.

"No."

Somehow I was up, I stood and worked my legs.

I opened the door. The light of the hall hurt my eyes.

Mr. Coughlan like a ghost if not for the light, if not for his solicitousness. Mr. Coughlan apologizing. His door was locked. He did not remember locking it, and while he had one key, the other wasn't on hand. Could I perhaps help? He'd been traveling and now . . .

Mr. Coughlan back again.

Life could be benevolent. I'd forgotten. A reversal. Mr. Coughlan here: as surprising and unlikely as Melville's captain surviving his obsession or, better, Odysseus's return after so many years and trials met. Life making returns— returned loved ones, returning with them, to you, a part of yourself you did not know how much you missed. His face before me, set on mine, one covered in tributaries of red rushing through and around patches of brown, beautiful scars, whitened nicks and deep scores as if he shaved on choppy waters too often or had liked to put his face in the gale, never-minding the consequences. How gorgeous scars can become once you've survived them or when in some fashion you choose them, and would again.

Was that what we were missing through the collecting of our disappointments, that life had as many gains as losses as long as we were willing to tally them, each side, with clear-sightedness? But were we ever clear and did we often seek to be? I was clear enough at seeing him to throw my arms around him to hold him there, to make sure I was not dreaming him up, my ferryman always in motion, wind on him even now, a chill on his clothes. I held on to that, too, and the smells of ash and salt all over him. Where have you been? Where? Where?

It was Les who said give the man some room, let him breathe, but Les was already fading. Les no longer mattered, and he knew it. The battle was over, its spell. Brazo came as Les was leaving, forgetting his expensive bouquets. Brazo standing in my hall upright with alarm, his limbs itchy and alert with blood. A protector by nature and trade, ticking. A man good in crises, who thrives in them. "You think it's wise to come back here, buddy? You think you can just go anywhere you want, huh?" Les stared him down briefly, snorted a little, and, brushing past the detective, was gone. Like that. More than merely subdued— vanished.

Brazo stepped closer, leading with his long nose to the real object of his interest: "I've been tracking you, sir."

"Whatever for?" said Mr. Coughlan, genuinely surprised.

"Your daughter and your landlady here. They were concerned. A report was filed."

Coughlan breathed out and scratched loudly at the back of his head: "My daughter makes a life out of worrying. That's probably my fault." He drifted for a moment thinking of it, then rubbed his eyes as if they were full of grit, and blew out another sigh. "But I am sorry. I'll tell her, and let me convey it to you, Miss Cassill. I didn't want to worry anyone. I wasn't coming back till I looked into a few things. I couldn't stay put anymore." He searched my face while forming a grimace that meant to be a smile. "Now I need to rest. I'm tired." And having admitted it, his posture untied and drooped. He raised a hand, not high. "Thank you both."

"I have to call your daughter. And maybe a doctor?" Brazo said.

"Tell her I am going to bed. And I'm not paying for any doctor. There's nothing wrong with me but old age and I've got that beat for now." With effort he twisted his shoulders toward the stairs. I ducked in to get his key.

He stood before the stairs when I came out.

"Wouldn't the elevator be——" I started.

But he'd taken the first step up. Maybe because Brazo was there or maybe because this was the last test in a series he'd set for himself, that coming back had to be earned just like everything else, he would take the stairs to the top. He did not hurry, couldn't, and only half-noticed that Brazo and I trailed behind.

"You were in Maryland two, three days ago. You took the bus there. How did you get back?"

"By boat. Ship . . . Cargo."

We listened to him breathe every step, to the effort of his joints.

"What sort of cargo?"

A step considered, climbed, then another: "Old men," he said.

"C'mon."

Finally, on the landing of the third floor as he was sizing up the next and last flight, he answered without looking at us: "Cargo was old man and some lumber."

We waited with him and then having taken one, then another step, he paused again. "I wanted to see if an old man could find work."

"Were you able to?" I asked.

"Yes and no. Everyone fears a man my age." He turned from two steps up and took inventory of me once more, my eyes, my mouth, as if to make certain I was all there. And then looked Brazo over, the size of his hands and shoes, the dense black of his hair: "Liability. A man my age."

The very last of the stairs were accomplished efficiently and quietly to underscore his point—he was no one's weak link, no matter how worn.

I unlocked the door and switched the light on for him. Only one bare bulb responded, a sore-making light. Without permission I scooted in first. I cracked the window nearest the harbor, to let in the ferry sounds, the night and its rain now, yes, raising the mineral smells of the season. I put fingers to the radiator, which was warm but not too hot on an April evening that promised to be no colder than fifty degrees. It wasn't such a bad place after all, was it? Warm and dry? And out of the rain?

"I thank you both—" His voice wavered, went out. "I thank you both," he uttered again, clearing his throat, and extended his coarsened hand to each of us, as if I had not hugged him and fussed, as if we'd lost reality for him once more, "and now, if I might, I must rest."

Outside his door, the two of us alone, Brazo and I turned shy.

"Well, he's home, safe and sound," he said, but he didn't smile and his words were slack, and he blinked and blinked under his heavy, live brow, because I guessed he felt as I did, that he wanted more: We wanted a meal of him; we wanted him to tell us stories, wag his head, his calloused fingers at us; to raise a glass for homecomings, for our worry, how needless it had been after all; we wanted to be comforted, we didn't want a door between us and for him to disappear again.

"Yes, a happy ending," I agreed.

A CITY ARRANGEMENT

———

HOPE ASKED, AT NOON, when she came for me, if I was okay.

"Just tired," I told her, but finally resigned and so calmer in a way I hadn't been all through the night. The rain had come and stayed. And the thunder—so long it had lasted, more than an hour, two, rumbling low and long like god's vast empty stomach hanging over us, me. I was queasy well until the morning, motion sick from one man's return, others going, gone—Brazo looking momentarily unsure of his balance, telling me *take care* before wandering off— and of course from my having let the alcohol run into me without the care of food or water or other insulation. I directed myself to stay in my bed through the night and then was up opening the windows to the rain, cold April rain, and back again and up again, riding the motion, arguing with myself that all was well. It's true that twice I went to Coughlan's door to see if he was still there, part of the argument with myself. The first time at one o'clock, roughly, opening his door a crack to hear him, if he could be heard, and he could be, still there, asleep and issuing robust scouring breaths. And when I woke with a start at 4 or 5 A.M., I got up and dressed for the rain, which had reduced to misting, the thunder passed. I went to an all-night market for groceries: a loaf of bread; two ripe tomatoes; four spotless bananas; eight cans of soup; five cans of tuna; cold cuts; a dozen eggs; a quart of milk; mayonnaise; as much as I could carry, as much as would sustain him up there.

I knocked this time, so I could be heard, but not enough to startle him. He did not answer. I knocked again. Then I went in, whispering, "Hello, hello? . . ." Hissing with my version of a landlady's cheer done in a whisper, "I'm sorry to disturb, I have food for you, to welcome you back . . ." to hear him still snoring heartily in his bedroom—the most gorgeous sound. I then put the perishables in the fridge; the rest I left on the counter for him. And having made my delivery, I still worried but less, and I slept till the light found my face and roused me. The sun was back and I readied myself for Hope.

———

"It's best if you dress for mess," she said when she arrived. Then laughed: "We're sort of going back in time. Clearing up."

I was wearing nothing that I worried about ruining and so we set out, lightly bumping into one another, as we moved into the hall, brushing arms, once, then twice, as we got in step into an outside shining with puddles, wet trees, slick bark, and leaves sodden and plump, still so newly and freshly green it was hard not to put them in your mouth. I wanted to remark this to Hope, who was telling me about Darren and Josephina, a quarrel over the Hamptons, Josephina saying all the wealth there has impoverished the place of its beauty. She was laughing again, head high, quoting them ("So few public places," Josephina had said, "so few wild"). Of course I remembered Les telling me that Hope knew I'd gone into her apartment. I'd been waiting for it to come up, but what was clear as she distracted us with conversation was that if she did know, she never cared. All her resources and queries were dedicated elsewhere.

She looped her arm in mine, pulling me to her. She couldn't know that when she did, with the smell of her invading, how immediately and irrepressibly I recalled her body. What a beautiful woman I had been permitted to travel, cave deep, survival hard, a purple bruise on the crook of her arm where the IV had gone in during her hospital stay, a scar above her pubis, another on her knee, skin knotted,

tight and then loose. A complicated landscape. No two
women the same . . . But as we walked she couldn't have
known. She couldn't be blamed. If she trapped any details
of my body, any evidence of its or my reality, it was only
to stop seeing the loss for a time, a reprieve, but I'd already
been floated away, even as I kept pace with her long strides
and she spoke in lists: *Darren wants what everyone else has. Josephina scoffs at what everyone wants. My daughter wants everyone
to want her, and to think of her wants first. My son tries not to
want too much, tries not to be disappointed.* I should have volunteered, "Me, too. I'm like Leo," but I'd not earned my
place on her lists, and I was tired and intoxicated, too,
even as I understood I was a comfort, one easily enough
replaced, as she'd replaced Les, valuable largely for my
willingness to do what she needed now, not to say no to
her. And why would I? That my fingers knew her, corners
and textures, patchwork and depths, that she held my arm
in hers as we walked now, so that I could see outside me,
to her regal profile, to the wet, verdant streets of Brooklyn, the uneven pavement and faces passing us, it was yet a
pleasant dislocation. And I looked to see who looked at her,
whose oblivion to passersby was nearly total (to New York-
ers who avoid eye contact or risk becoming oversaturated
in the effort to trap things and faces familiar and unfamiliar,
that are often gone before they've arrived). And it was true
that despite themselves they looked, at her amiable hauteur,
her purpose. How could they not?

All these years she only lived a mere seven blocks from

me, into Cobble Hill, in a stately four-story town house I'd admired for its Gothic Revival touches—the cast-iron railings and metalwork gas lanterns to either side of its grand arched Tudor doorway, an imperturbable front. We were stalled outside as she considered it and what she might find inside.

"He's not home?" I asked.

"No."

"Does he know you're coming?"

"Yes. To collect some things. He's at work, but to be on the safe side I asked that he not be here as a courtesy to me."

As she unlocked the door, she said, "We deal in courtesies. I have to try or else kill him."

Through the door, there was lustrous wide timber on the floor already, an oriental runner in braiding browns and blues which led to the base of a staircase of painted white wood that curved up and away like a swan's neck.

She stood at the living room's threshold and made more lists, out loud, as introductions for me and probably as an act of reclamation for her. The sunlight surged through the tall windows, making it all glow in collusion with her list-making: Bergère chairs and an ottoman, another oriental in coral and sage, and "in there"—her hand lifted to indicate the dining room—an Aubusson rug gotten at a reduced price in the South of France because of the slightest flaw, "imperceptible really," she said, a chandelier from Murano, where "we visited on our honeymoon." "He never refused me anything or not in a long time. We stopped worrying about money years ago." Lamps with beaded shades, fat gilded frames and the paintings they contained, the odd bits of sculpture—a disembodied hand, a bust, a Buddha—even driftwood on the marble-mouthed mantel of the fireplace (a touch of her shabby chicness where France met the American seaside). The majority of these things were older than she was and yet were brought to life, breathing and contemporary because of how she'd arranged them, and even the most austere pieces—"this is a Restoration secretary"—were disarmed by a countryscape hung over it done in chewy impressions or a fraying basket stuffed with weary yarn—"I knit when I think of it." Books were laid out on the coffee table, some distressed with age, others as shiny and expensive as appliances, like gaudy memorials to their subjects. The ceilings on the parlor floor had to be fourteen or fifteen feet high, the moldings intricate and paneled on the front and rear walls of the long room.

"It's otherworldly," I said, awed to foolishness and ready to admit I thought a place like this an impossibility in New York—a home so spacious and, whenever it required it, quiet; I heard no footfalls, no car traffic, no ferry horns. Over time I no longer could conceive of a place without warrens for solitary bodies because that's all I could conceive for myself now—a body alone and mostly wanting to be. But the house I'd grown up in had been like this, with rooms that promised expanse and as many chairs, tables, plates, and glasses as needed for social gatherings, dizzyingly bright with natural or manufactured light, with improvisation, and lousy with art gotten through family, auctions, galleries, filthy antique shops, elegantly contrary—an Asian scroll painting of bird and bamboo beside an English seascape. My mother like Hope was in charge of a room's currents and conversations. Yes, this was Hope's own, all of it, a live tribute to her powers and tastes, the drive to have taste in fact, the right to it.

She'd left me at the threshold to pick up an empty glass left on a coaster on her coffee table in the middle of the room. She held the glass to the light—a half-moon of lipstick.

Laughter, full of shards: "Do you think he left this out for me to see?"

"I don't know," I said.

She laughed again in a way that sounded like it pained her.

"Could it be your daughter's?"

"Oh, I doubt it. She'd never wear such a horrid shade of pink."

She set the glass back down with mechanical care as if she were exhorting herself not to break it.

She surveyed the room and hugged her arms around her chest, and I observed something go out in her eyes—where I saw love and admirable confidence in every choice she'd made to make this room, and surely this whole house, what it was, she saw the magic that bound it together and to her evaporating before her.

"This is all you," I told her, because its truth seemed so

obvious to me. "He's living with you, whether you're here or not."

Lines formed in trenches in her brow, and her mouth became tiny as if she was struggling not to spit something out.

"That's why he can do it, Hope. You're his foundation, even now, what he's pushing off from."

"This is already gone," she said simply. "All this, but until then it's the garden we have to contend with. Come."

She led me to a wide porch overlooking a yard two to three times the size of my own. A privilege she had not wasted, a long-standing arrangement between her and nature in a city so stingy with nature held privately.

"A gardener did this?"

"Me," she said. "I'm the gardener."

"No help?"

"Some in the beginning and occasionally I'd call in reinforcements for the weeding, a friend, my kids, but mostly it's me. I feel no-account if I'm not managing it on my own."

The yard was as generous a space as the footprint of her brownstone. Two estuaries of flat blue stone ran down the level length of it, creating thick rising beds to either side. Between the paths was a swath of grass fresh as a river and every day more so, its plushness and volume the new season's. In the middle of the grass was a weathered stone birdbath fountain, in two tiers; it had not been turned on yet and it sat on a circular bed of soil broken by shoots and blossoms. Toward the rear of the yard was an old cedar gazebo, small for a gazebo in that it would seat two or maybe three and was handmade from the delicate look of it, listing under a thicket of vines covering it. Behind it, reaching to the yard's corners were trees, a tall birch unfurling itself thirty feet or more to the sky; another tree's blue-green leaves looked maple, but its bark was cinnamon-colored and its base made up of not one trunk but many dividing trunks spreading out like a hand to keep what was private private; then on the other side next to a stolid evergreen there stood an astonishment of fine white blossoms that comprised a tree of fifteen or so feet.

"That tree there, with the white——"

"A Japanese plum," she told me.

"Wow."

"Yes . . . He saw it in China first years ago—that's where they originated, not Japan—and then I think he saw it again in a garden in England during his business trips, so many trips he's taken." She was merely reciting now, not editorializing. "And he thought of me each time he saw one. He was amazed to find the tree for sale here, as if it couldn't travel. He didn't know the Botanic Garden has them, like an *army* of them. And it wards off evil or that's the story. Plant it in the northeast, they say, because that's the direction evil comes from. He said it was our duty to grow it and keep it well—to protect us." She took time to look at it. "It's sensitive. It didn't thrive at first. I took it personally."

And then: "You know, I didn't garden as a kid. My mother

did. My father, too. He liked to help. I wasn't at all interested and now I sometimes wake up worrying about what the frost may do. I had no idea I'd take to it as I did or how gratifying I'd find it out here."

I remembered a line from *Here Is New York*, a pleasing compact send-up of the city by E. B. White. A Connecticut neighbor sent it to me when I first moved to New York, and one of White's pronouncements had stayed with me ever since: "No one should come to New York to live unless he is willing to be lucky." I thought I was willing back then, and now standing on Hope's porch, as on a prow of a ship, I was reminded that both of us had invested all our luck in whom we'd chosen to love, to align our lives with. Our husbands were both men who had ambition for making money, had no shame in its pursuit, in a crowded field of commerce, in constant and unforgiving competition. Her husband had survived, and to anyone's eyes, it would appear Hope had gone so much farther in her commitment to their life together than I had; I hadn't had the same chances and maybe I wouldn't have had the same drive to nourish dynamic life into the income my husband had generated as Hope had—an extraordinary home, two feeling children, a garden that made demands she was happy to answer for; she'd given all her imagination to it, and in the lists she was making for me again now were all the evidence of that commitment, how fluently she was naming the parts, pointing to daffodils *there,* common primrose, hellebore—*do you see it from here, it's just up?*—crocuses, violets, grape hyacinth, tulips—"those bloom early," she said, "those over there do not"—some plantings visible, alive for weeks: yes, modest tulips, yellow and slender, yet so tightly held in April, others gapping already, showing us the color of their insides—brash and kaleidoscopic in their honesty. There were plants and flowers still waiting to greet her under the soil; and she named these, too: hosta, lamb's ear, blue fescue, moor grass, foxglove, "which is so temperamental, it grows in stages and only lasts about two seasons but *what* color . . ." or waiting within the lines of their branches: "That's a paperback maple. Its red skin looks so stunning in the snow. I planted it when we bought this place twenty years ago. And that," she looked at the gazebo, "will be covered in clematis . . . ." Her commitment set in motion, renewing itself in agreement with the seasons every year, yes, flattering her choices and her hard work, like dreams coming true over and over. Now with listless wonder she told me: "We used to say we had the whole world back here."

And it was a wonder: Spring performing for her when she could not help but feel winter all through her, a bruise on her arm where the IV had been, Les only a week ago fucking her to break her in two.

"I have gloves, clippers and scissors, wheelbarrows, a cart and a wagon. I have aprons and hats and some dirty towels. I have plenty of pots. We'll replant what we can in your garden. What we can't replant we'll cut for bouquets, which we can give as gifts or keep for ourselves.

We'll dig up all of it or most of it. What we can't dig up, we'll shear."

"Dig it up? Why?" I asked, dumbfounded.

"He's destroyed something."

"He has."

"And I'm making him see the casualties firsthand."

"But you created this. It's your work."

"And I can undo it. I can't say that about most things." The sky was empty of clouds and blue and bright, and she led me down the iron stairs to her tools and supplies.

My first response was no, we can't, it's simply too lovely, but I watched her unlock her shed and carry out all that we'd need with incredible calm. She was silent and sure and created an atmosphere of a woman determined and I wanted to live in that, join her there for as long as I could, more finally than I cared about the fate of her flowers, or even her trees. They say expectations of an experience guide and distort that experience. I had had none coming here. I had no real desire to say yes or no, to choose between those options, as life requires of us over and over. I had only a disposition to be partnered in something of consequence to someone I cared for and who in this moment anyway cared for me. Here, today, I could tell my mother I was not merely a spy. And I wasn't afraid: I took up the clippers and cut the opened tulips clear through at the stem, letting them fall heavy-headed, and dug up the others and sat them in a pot of soil for replanting as I saw Hope do. She instructed by doing and gave me what I'd really been after: belonging somewhere that soon enough was a place outside simple time or anywhere recognizable to me, because we lost time together, as we set to work in the wet soil. We divided into halves, our most fundamental parts, as adults often do; we were the children we never stop being, marveling at the mud—fibrous, peaty, sandy, claylike—and also women worrying for it, negotiating with our worry, dirt in every crease, under every fingernail, in our hair, damp through to our knees already. We did not speak, for if we did we might falter and lose the urgency necessary to undo this world of Hope's, a sanctuary that for so long she controlled but couldn't anymore; and her stabbing the soil with her shovel, turning over the beds, was both her acceptance of and her rebellion against what wasn't hers anymore, of what, as she said, was already gone.

We filled over a dozen clay and plastic pots with plants and flowers to transplant and placed the cut flowers in her wheelbarrow. I'd chosen to take off my gloves because I was clumsy in them so had grasped the roots and filaments, pebbles and bulbs as I pulled them that felt in the hand like mammals' veins and loose male genitals and tumors and plum pits. We worked efficiently and savagely, it was true, making our decision about what to preserve and what not to without fussing or consulting our consciences or one another, and so it took me longer than it should have to notice her hands were bleeding as she struck the soil to unearth the Japanese plum's roots, assessing just how deep and far they reached. She'd taken off her gloves, too; maybe they were slipping or maybe like me she eschewed any barrier between her and the day's intentions. Of course I had to stop her from hurting herself, and I saw myself get up and put a hand on her lower back, but in fact I didn't move—it would break the spell. I waited until the violence I felt made the choice for me, for it was all through me and Hope surely; it had to be to do what we were doing. The black, black soil mostly empty now, and wanting, was like an invitation.

"I didn't tell you. I meant to," I called to her over her heavy breathing and the shovel's grunts. "That tenant of mine, the ferry captain, I may have told you about him? He came home last night. He'd been gone for weeks. Mr. Coughlan? I'd been worried and had thought he'd never come back and then he appeared at my door. He arrived just as Les was leaving."

She straightened and, still breathing hard, looked at me as if she'd forgotten all about me or at least about speech and, marveling at the lapse, searched for decorum. "You let him in, after he came to me, did you?"

"Les? I opened the door so he'd quit beating on it."

She gave out a loose laugh and sighed. She saw her hands and the state of them and laughed again. "My God . . . He doesn't learn. Well, so, did he behave?"

"No."

"Did you?"

"I didn't hit him this time. I invited him in. I certainly didn't want him to stay, but he—"

"He imposes," she said.

"Yes."

"And sometimes it's good." She surveyed the ground, then looked up at all the tree's blossoms, squinted at the sky.

"Yes," I agreed.

She leaned her shovel against the fence. "And sometimes it's not."

"Yes." And because alone with her I was possessive and gleeful in a way I could barely disguise, I looked to kill him again, but this time it was his chance with her, any future for them that I was after, and so I said, "He's an animal."

But she resurrected him. "We all are, darling. Animals. We've all done things we're ashamed of, but we survive. Or most of us." She wiped her hands on her khakis, staining them. "I don't think I can dig this tree up, or not without brawn; that means a few tree men. It's just too big now. Do you want it at your place very much?"

I did want it suddenly, terribly, this part of Hope and her husband's life, but I did not trust the lust in my heart, and Hope had just put me in my place rather neatly. I thought of my own little yard, which had never been mastered because I hadn't wanted to. I wanted something of that wildness that I'd known only moments ago, before I'd broken the spell. I wanted to be surprised.

And I was. Less than a week later, Angie appeared at my door with a printed invitation from Hope and me in one hand and a stout bouquet of daffodils in the other. She held

them up for a moment so I could see and then lowered
them.

"A party?"

I confirmed it. She did not interrogate me, restraining,
for now, her uncomfortable-making curiosity. The party
was a pretense for coming down. Her voice was thin. I
could see, though her face was flushed and her mole bright
and beating with the blood all through her, that she was
working on a problem inside her and all her resources were
there. She clasped her hands over her stomach, covering it
with the flowers and the invitation, an odd enactment of
composure.

"There doesn't seem to be hot water or not much."

The past several days had been unseasonably warm for
April, and the boiler, my centrifuge, my friend, stopped
making heat just as it should, but its thermostat was too
sensitive, a design flaw I'd meant to address, and it told
the equipment to go too far—no hot water. A rare thing
but not unheard of during a change of seasons when even
dead wood swells and sweats, has complaints. It had happened last spring, but I had noticed before anyone else and
so did not hold the boiler or me accountable or even remember till now.

It was barely 7:30 in the morning. I told her I'd go directly. Apologized. Landlords must be prepared to apologize
as much as possible; it needs to be the punctuation to every
reply to a tenant or nearly. But Angie did not seem to hear.

She had jeans and flip-flops on under a stiff white cotton

nightgown, the stuff of choirs and virgins. I moved to go, but she was not quite ready to let me.

"The invitations are printed and embossed. This paper is recycled and pretty expensive. You paid for them to be printed? For this party, out there in your yard?"

"No, not me. Hope, the woman who is subletting George's place."

She nodded.

I said, "The flowers are from her garden."

Absent, she nodded again.

"We replanted a lot in my yard." And we had—it took two days, a sunburn, sore hands, necks, and backs, and a decision to leave her Japanese plum behind. "You'll see if you come to the party."

Even this information did not catch in her. What notice she'd taken of the building's newest occupant and what questions she had about her didn't matter now. Angie tacked there, squeezing her full hands into her stomach over her gown now, rubbing slightly, crushing the daffodil stems, then making an effort to stop herself. I knew then, I suppose, or maybe just before, grace of what? The warmer days, sensations new to me, the beautiful circuity of recent events? Yes, I felt Angie's physicality between us like a mass of breathing vines taking over, gorgeous and sightless and frightening in their intelligence and direction. I knew before she told me, which she did: "I'm pregnant."

"Well, then . . ." I said. And was lost, too, calculating for her all the ramifications. Mitchell gone. I didn't congratulate her. I offered, "Well, then, you'll be needing hot water."

She looked at me for the first time and laughed in an uneven puff of air that got away from her, then stopped herself abruptly.

"Big news." I grinned, and when her face did not reply in kind, I stopped.

"Yes," she said.

"Not planned," I said.

She shook her head. Bewilderment the color of yellow rose up from inside her or from the daffodils reflecting up into her sea-glass green eyes. She stared down at the flowers, concentrating, talking herself out of tears or more. She breathed her big bosom up and down, up and even deeper down.

"There are flowers in front of every apartment," she said. "Left with the invitation."

"Hope. She's very excited about the party. Will you come?"

She became exasperated then—I was obfuscating, wandering from the matter at hand, and the world was too altered, flowers in front of every door! Some woman let loose in our halls. "My *god,* Celia. I don't know! I don't know. I just don't—" She pushed the ragged bouquet and the invitation at me, into my hands, and then, at a loss, put her hands on her hips that may have not felt quite like hers, only to let her limbs drop as far as they would go, not far.

Small arms, small hands. She'd probably never felt so small. She closed her eyes. Steadying herself.

"That man, our neighbor, is back, isn't he? I can hear him walking over me. He's okay?"

"Mr. Coughlan? Upstairs? Yes."

"I don't know whether to tell him," she said.

"Mr. Coughlan?"

"No." She opened her eyes to scold me with her regard. "*Mitchell,* who else?"

I felt the invitation in my hand, the texture of the stiff ivory paper. Hope had shown it to me with the trill of a bride-to-be—"It fits the event perfectly, doesn't it?" she said. "So simple and elegant and full of the season—I couldn't resist. And I'm going to cook for days . . ." The fullness of her excitement had surprised me. With her garden as she had composed it gone but for where it was preserved in her mind, for her to map all alone, she'd been made lighter, and like a girl rushing to share her fantasy of how one greets the spring with adults who badly needed to be reminded, she insisted on leaving bundles of flowers tied in a cotton string at every door, even her own and mine—we could not be left out, after all. Her happiness at the prospect of what was to come, a party to begin, curled into the building, into the lines of the leaves pushing and squeaking at the windows, and into me, too. How could I tell Angie what I'd seen—that a woman embarked finally on something new, giddy with courage, could mean everything? And in the last few days the mouth of my back-yard had been opened so it would take in all the flowering plants we had for it; roots snug in foreign clots of dirt were secured in its soil and in new soil brought in in bags dense as bodies. Yes, its mouth was full and could speak only of abundance. I had not foreseen how transformed it would feel. How to explain to Angie that you could love what you could not foresee, that we are all shape-shifting whether we want to or not? Hope put her married name on the in-vite, alongside mine, Boxer and Cassill. They were our names after all, even if the men who'd given them to us were not anymore or not in the way we'd imagined.

"You have to tell him, Angie. You were a family, the two of you, right?"

"Yes."

"And he's always wanted this?"

"Yes, of course, yes, but he'll come back for the baby. I want him to come back for me."

"Tell him that, too."

"I'm—" She touched her stomach again. She might have said exhausted, scared. I could see both. Or disap-pointed. I saw that there, too, or I think I did. I saw it ev-erywhere if I chose to. I handed the daffodils, the invitation back to her.

"Hot water will improve things. . . . Let me attend to it now—" I reached out to touch her arm, but she'd al-ready moved off, toward the stairs.

"Thank you," she said, gone into a fog again of scenarios, conversations, conflicts.

"Provisions have to be made," I called to her. "And some improvisation is required. You don't have to be together to be parents together. And there are other forms of support, other people out there just waiting to be in a family—"

She didn't believe me so the words just dissolved, flimsy, no matter my conviction. Her small round back to me, she sighed, found another mechanical thank-you and went up and away as I made for the boiler, something I knew how to care for, something that even in its failures didn't surprise me.

I'LL WAIT FOR YOU

———

WHAT I HAD KNOWN of happiness was that it sat best in small cups; it was designed for the sprinter or the wave destroying itself on the rocks; it couldn't be clutched at or too carefully observed; and its departure couldn't be guessed at; but still the day of the party I tried to charm it with bargains, promises; if it would stay just long enough, I would do anything.

On that day, a Saturday, from mid-morning to late afternoon feet scrambled overhead, as if in gossipy conversation with one another. Hope came in and out of my apartment as did her children and her friends, each toting something for her or for the party, a gift of wine—sparkling, pink, white, red—thick cloth table napkins, paper lanterns to hang from the trees so we could brave the dark when it came; they rolled a grill the size of an old jukebox on wheels seven blocks from Hope's former home. (Darren, I was told, wanted to christen it with champagne. Expensive champagne. Hope would have let him, but Josephina would not.) I'd insisted on contributing cash for my part in the food and rented the tables and chairs, swept and bought white candles. I found a dress almost the color of Angie's eyes and made for a long neck like Hope's. Its neckline scooped and its cool summer cotton followed me closely from my breasts down across my stomach and hips before it flared gently and told anyone who cared to look that the shape of me had nothing to hide. When I put it on, it brushed against the back of my knees to remind them what it was to be bare so I took it off, only to put it back on again. The air was fresh, its temperature circling seventy; the light was lemony and mixed with clouds bright and sluggish and as top-heavy as mountains.

"I've never seen you in a dress," Hope said, carrying in supplies hidden in Tupperware for storing in my fridge. The free fingers of her right hand, which was bandaged around her palm from our exertions, absently traced my rib cage and waist as she fell into reporting on the food she'd prepared: foie gras arancini, pan-fried baby artichokes and arugula with lemon aioli, quail egg canapés. And cheese, of course cheese: Hudson Valley Camembert, Grafton three-year cheddar, Nettle Meadow Kunik (*Kunik? A triple crème cheese made from goat and cow's milk,* she explained, *it will get you high, it's so good; I'm* not *kidding*). Grapes, walnuts, and baguette, not crackers, *never* crackers; soufflé aux épinards (*you know that's spinach of course*), a roasted trout with herbs and lemon for the non-meat-eaters, and for the omnivores, a baby rack of lamb. And mussels. *An enormous bowl.* There would be sparkling water and lemonade; and Muscadet for the mussels. *Sancerre goes with pretty much everything and there's Châteauneuf-du-Pape for the lamb. My son grills with the patience of a civil servant.* She'd chosen Gosset Rosé Champagne—*to drink with the dessert or anything else*—fruit tart and petits pots de crème in ginger, passion fruit, and noisette—noisette? *Hazelnut, you silly. You know that.* Yes, I did, but I wanted her to tell me, to slow her down. *Please, slow down.* But I did not say that out loud, to her or the day. I simply wished for it.

"I think it will be enough, don't you? But will your tenants like it—they are coming? Oh, I hope so. The party's for them as much as anyone else. And for them to see your garden. Won't they be amazed? That sweet plump girl on the floor above me—I saw her in passing just yesterday. She looked like a motherless child."

I wanted to elaborate and remark on the uncanniness of the comment, but already she was on to scaling other visions, aiming so high, announcing, "New air! How do you get it? Travel! George was showing me the way, but I wasn't ready to see it then, but now where won't I go? Why hadn't I thought of it sooner? I have friends in Rome, Berlin, Brittany—oh, that rough coast! You have to see it, if you haven't. And Turkey. I've been meaning to go for years. And Rome? Have you been? The colors of the old stucco structures—these pinks and yellows and nutty oranges— and the texture of the walls and roofs. My god, it's like this labyrinth of ruins that shouldn't be standing but they do, and with more solidity and grace than us, that's for sure, and palm trees! Can you imagine?! Palm trees in the midst of this ancient Western city, the most impermanent sort of tree, don't you think? And I read just recently that there's some insect eating up those Roman palms, and you know the Italians won't do a thing about it. Not so long ago now, Leo got on the bus in Rome with an expired ticket— without realizing of course—and the police who came on doing their fare checks took him off and told him fifty euro or prison. He paid them. Oh, it's corrupt, that city, and lazy but glorious and overpowering. Meet me there? Why not?" She poured us both a taste of the champagne. "Or the Amalfi Coast?" Then she sighed herself into stillness, temporary, and drained her glass. "I won't force you. You think about it. Let's not get ahead of ourselves. I wouldn't want to be, well . . ." She peered into her trip, a woman traveling by herself, perhaps seeing herself at a café taking espresso alone, or a glass of wine. "Men will look at me with pity but not all. Some women too, but if I want company and I may not, but *if* and when I do, I'll look for the exceptions. Like you," she said, turning to me and fitting her injured hand around the contour of my cheek with the plain affection of an older sister. Still goose bumps rose all over me like children jumping up to put their faces in the sun, and I was half-drunk at noon, exhilarated and queasy, certain already that the day and its gifts—and maybe its consequences, too—were greater than my ability to meet them.

I said very little as I finished my champagne but smiled and nodded and gave yes-yes's, thrilling to all of it with her. To meet her wherever she went or to tell her, as I wanted to more than once, *please stay a while longer, Hope,* to tell her anything more of my heart would mean sooner or later to tell her everything, what I'd chosen, who I'd chosen and still chose. To tell her, even five years after the fact, still felt a betrayal of all that I consented to on the last day of my husband's life. You see, once I agreed to give him all the morphine he needed to die on a burning hot July day, a day so long that sometimes it felt I was still living it, once I agreed to let him go because his body had turned cruel and was tired and empty and leaking, I promised to restore him as he'd been. It wasn't just a sentimental promise to my husband, who was so bitterly ashamed of dying when all he longed to do was live, but a promise I made to me, in order to survive what I agreed to do that day and then carried out. But it's never so simple as all that. The body does not want to die. His breaths—I counted them until I couldn't. They sounded hard-edged, they crackled inside him, dragged and plowed and wheezed—hundreds I counted, one more ragged than the next. He was hooked to a morphine drip, Helen had seen to that part, a baseline prescribed by a doctor. The extra, also prescribed as supplement to the IV, as needed, was given from a dropper; he sucked from it like a teat, but he had difficulty swallowing and choked. Broken blood vessels, petechiae, knit inside his eyes, around them from choking. And those breaths still came. Yes, the body wants to live, but my husband did not. *C'mon, baby. C'mon. Enough of this before it takes us both with it.* I took on the obligation that day to his stronger self, to all we'd had in store—children, travel, outsize freedom from everyday tedium—and to how much faith there was between us. Daphne, my childhood friend, hadn't chosen her love well. She'd let it choose her. I had chosen well, and I'd prove it with my strength, my loyalty; and those breaths that kept coming were an affront to that choice, of him, one that I would make again, even with the illness, to a man who wanted to love me and be loved by me for so much longer than we were allowed. Those breaths wouldn't stop even after I injected him—more morphine. He was not conscious, he could not hold my hand or feel my body cupped around his in that rented metal bed. I stood up—and my heart, the room, the very air began to speed up as I did—I stood up and took a pillow encased in a plain blue pillowcase and, everything moving now, with my own gaudy heartbeat, faster, too fast for uncertainty, I pressed it over those unconscious, unwanted breaths. Helen had not instructed me on this—only on the overdose, how to do it, over how much time, where to inject him if necessary, but you see I recognized that calm of Hope's, the one she showed me in her garden, because I had had it once. I stopped those breaths that would not stop, and once I did that I owed him all of me every day, alive so he could be. That was how it had come to feel. At first, finding myself alone in that room, the shock had made me run. I could not contain the pain those first weeks. The guilt. I wanted to go with him. Obliterate me. But there was no going back and finally that choice, that day, and every choice that followed it, this building, the prayer for an orderly place, these tenants, even Hope and what we had stumbled into, would mean nothing if I did not keep him well, his youthful self, like a flame inside me, clarifying and burning. I had no choice, and I still didn't.

GOODBYE FOR NOW

———

THE YELLOW TABLECLOTH flew up and over the tables pushed together into the long, rigid backbone of a banquet. The chairs, some dozen, filled with bodies—so fast was the party populating and cheeks craning for the brush of lips, hands shaking, reaching for food, plates clacking, bottles hoisted and handled hard. One glass broke and quickly was swept up; it vanished into the relay of speech, words sent out as sentries, flares. Look here! Look at me! And this food! *Oh, my god, what is in my mouth, Hope?! Hope, you sorceress!* Effusive and at erratic speeds, as if our chances to be seen and heard were diminishing before us and we had to hurry. Ten people at table with their mouths moving, in a yard that had rarely seen more than one or two visitors at a time.

Josephina had brought an artist friend named Jorge from Barcelona; Danielle had invited a boyfriend or a prospective one—I was not sure. And the flowers we'd planted crowded in around us, as if desperate to participate, some bending, dying already from the shock of their move. They suffocated me in their colors and number—how they instructed on perishability. My lilac bush was obscured in the thicket but fought for its pride of place with its full scent; my ginkgo and my sycamore seemed as shy as me, surrounded too suddenly and too lushly.

Blake and Andrew brought show tunes on CD and asked me where the stereo was: I had moved the old machine, my husband's once, by the window.

"Anything Goes" soon barked at us, upbeat, egging us on.

"Oh, Patti LuPone! She's a fucking genius!" cried Darren.

Andrew sang along, "The world's gone mad today and good's bad today and black's white today and day's night today," while tossing an arm over Leo, addressing the words to him, pulling him to him, the glorious substance of a healthy young man, who had carried the plates down, the serving dishes, the flatware, the bottles, who had snuck traveling looks at me in my dress each time, stealing high, stealing low, and the last look hanging on for as long as it took him to work his vigorous lungs an extravagant slow cycle, and me, despite myself, feeling his regards like two-fingered caresses.

Angie landed at the party in increments as if side-stepping. Dazed, I did not hear the door that would have warned me of her arrival and did not see her at first—her whole makeup a frown and a fidget and so tinier than ever. Once I was sure she'd decided not to run, I stood from my seat, found my voice, announcing her to everyone: "One of my tenants, Angie! A crusader and a model tenant!"

Blake raised his glass. "Hoopla, to Angie the crusader! Wine for the crusader!"

"Food first," said Hope, opening her hands to Angie, who had rooted herself in place. "Why haven't we met properly before now? I've been subletting for weeks and weeks and it seems so odd we haven't spent time together. . . ." Hope, with some gentle tugging, maneuvered Angie to a chair, telling her about the food options—"Do you eat cheese? Quail eggs? Oh, yes, organic, humanely treated, I'm all for it . . ."—while talking on as if shame and its gravity had been banished from her constitution for good. "Well, I know why we haven't chatted. I've been a positive wreck. My husband and I are parting ways and, really—Angie, is it?—that's putting it delicately. . . ." Hope laughed, tall in her own dress, royal blue and belted and plunging with a full 1950s-style skirt; her hair piled into its high twist. Her lipstick a dark shock. Impeccable. The only perceptible makeup. The lines around her eyes creasing deeply with her admission, "Yes, it's been an endurance race, one I almost lost—"

The old Angie would have been fast to say "Me, too,"

and chimed away in kind or better, faster certainly, but Angie was round-eyed and, like all of us to varying degrees, prostrate before such charm, so generous you had to follow it attentively to believe it.

When Hope offered her wine, Angie finally spoke, "Oh, no. I can't now," and without thinking shielded her stomach with her hand.

"Don't tell me," Hope burst out, "you're expecting a—"

Angie blocked her, "I'm sure you've heard by now: They've raised the terrorist alert to orange—or I think it's orange, the color right below red. It's elevated, one step away from scrambling those fighter planes. The news is running all over the place with rumors or what they're calling unsubstantiated reports that the Brooklyn Bridge is the target."

"Really?" said Hope, repeating it to the table. "Did everyone hear? About the bridge?"

Blake called: "No one's leaving!"

"The colors dictate!" howled Josephina. "What power colors have today!"

Darren: "Let's all stay the night! We'll outwait those terrorists with wine and see the dawn together!"

"If there are much wines to keep us warmed," said Jorge's heavily accented voice, "I will stay here and make toastings to the terrorist: May he find his virgin wives and leave the bombs to Uncle Sam." He had the look of a happy derelict about him. His voluptuous hairy belly shoved through the front seam of his buttoned shirt; his English was rudimentary and rude (cheerfully): "Now I will eat this mussel of the sea as I would the muscle of a woman. To women!" He raised his glass, and Leo, out of duty to a guest, did too.

Hope huddled Angie to her: "They may seem like beasts, my friends, but they're very well-intentioned or most of them. . . ."

"It's very changed back here," I heard Angie say and it was.

The music, Cole Porter's, had Blake and Andrew taking turns singing verses to one another, leaving Leo to make for the grill.

Hope had disarmed Angie enough that now she was addressing herself, for privacy and from the noise, to Hope's ear, confessing, surely, letting every detail go. How easy it looked.

Danielle's guest, whose name was Jeff or Jess, resembled her, built with lines that were all straightaways ending in youthful jutting joints. But against Danielle and her porcelain skin, his tan was so deep and honeyed so early in the season that it was, more than anything else, the color of affluence. He grinned and nodded and laughed before a sentence or witticism was completely expressed, too ready to please all these adults, yet running over with opinions and self-promotion. He could be heard to say, "the Hamptons," and to me and Darren he said, "they are the cure given us for Manhattan."

"Do we need a cure?" asked Josephina and he only

laughed as he explained earnestly about the death of Wall Street as we've known it—9/11 showed just how defenseless we are, "We can't rely on the old systems. They're too corrupt frankly, too entrenched. And it's all illusion anyway, right? If a company's paper goes up or down? It's manipulated."

Danielle, a complicit member of his self-promotion team and more exuberant than I'd known her to be, reported to Darren and me, "He studied Mandarin Chinese at Yale. He's taking me to China this summer, just the two of us. Jess says high tech is our common language now, that we'll all be working for China—"

"We already are," he assured us, breaking in. "All we have is our high-tech companies left, where this country's money is hiding—the high-tech guys are just holding on to it, hedging their—"

Darren craned in. "How do I get some of that money, short of stealing it?"

"Investment. Good stock choices," said Jess.

"But Wall Street is dead?"

The young man chuckled nervously. "Well, it still has its place."

"And your father?" Darren spoke while chewing. "What does he do? Don't tell me he works in investments?"

Before Jess could answer, Hope reappeared, a hand on my shoulder. "Who will have fish? And who will have meat?"

Jorge and Josephina did not hear—they bickered in Spanish and the music worked in between us all, making for lapses. Jorge reached for Josephina's breast. She slapped his hand and then leaned across the table to me and Danielle to say, "If he were not so ravenous in bed, I would send him out on the street." In the glare of the sunlight, the black eyeliner ringing her black eyes looked costumey and tribal; it made everything she said grave and impossible to argue with.

"Would you turn that music down, please?" Hope called. Andrew did her bidding and the garden opened a shade—one less element stirring its contents into a froth for which I knew I had little stamina. I had nowhere to hide—there was no clear exit for me on this occasion. I had all but trapped myself here.

I had left my apartment door unlocked, as well as the door to the corridor beside my apartment; the corridor joined the front hall to the garden as an independent access for tenants. Whichever route you took, there were two doors to pass through, to get to us, but it was the corridor door on which Hope had written on a piece of paper in her looping, exclamatory script: "Party today! All welcome."

The music low, we could hear birds again, cars streaming on the nearby street, and we could hear a door opening and closing; we could hear footsteps making down the wooden floor. Darren's eyes widened at me, mine replied in kind. We were both thinking Les. *Of course, Les.*

But before us stood a reed of a man, his head too big for such an intersection of sinew, seen in his thin exposed arms and neck and guessed at elsewhere. It was Mitchell, nervous, balancing on the balls of his feet, carrying daisies and looking into a field of faces he did not recognize save mine and Angie's, though hers was blank with shock.

"Mitchell!" I declared.

"Oh, *this* is Mitchell?" said Hope.

"Who is Mitchell?" asked Darren.

"Angie's husband," I reported.

But Angie said nothing and stared at him and then away as if she did not want to believe in the sight of him. Had she told him she was pregnant after all? And was that why he'd come without warning? Or had the threat of terrorism made him sentimental?

"Sit right here by your wife," said Hope. She introduced herself, told him how glad she was he'd found us. "And you brought flowers. We are just lousy with flowers. Aren't we lucky?"

"I saw the sign," he said. "I came to see Angie. She wasn't home."

"She is home," I said. "She's home out here with all of us."

He barely glanced at me and extended the bouquet to Angie, who received it as if he had handed her exotica or a rabbit straight out of his ear.

Darren's shoulders folded in, in relief, and Hope, a marvel of social intelligence, set after describing the food in all its particulars again, meaning to distract from the couple who did not embrace or greet each other but sat each as ramrod as rockets waiting to launch. More wine was opened.

Danielle ran, as directed by her mother, to retrieve new courses from my kitchen. Leo sliced the lamb.

When Hope filled Darren's glass with Châteauneuf-du-Pape, he looped his hand in the belt of her dress to bring her near:

"Did you invite *him*?"

"This man?" Hope asked.

"Don't be coy," he said.

"If you mean, Les, no. He's not invited, Darren."

"That's not stopped him before."

She laughed as if delighted, maybe flattered, as if Les were merely an incorrigible adolescent, then shook her head, shook off that laughter, while watching me watch her. "He won't come. Not today. I've explained it to him: Things have changed."

But I knew, as Darren surely did, that things could change again. That man would never stop, couldn't. He was a constant in that way, of nature or chaos. His appetite, his forward motion in service of it, he couldn't best it, not at this stage in his life when he feared losing too much. To win on the terms he'd strategized—that was the ideal in which he was held, to which he aspired, and there was Hope at the center of it, giving it human meaning, beauty. She'd let him in, ostensibly to comfort her, and he too willingly became part of the assault. But it wasn't fear I felt so much as resignation: It could be anything or anyone, couldn't it? You had to wait only so long for the assault on your perception of

how things should go, of who you are, the disruptions, the
upsets and losses. It felt nearly impossible to stay the course,
whatever your course. Even our great bridge wasn't safe
today, and perhaps tomorrow: Armed men crawled all over
it; helicopters beat its piece of sky.

Angie had started weeping into the bouquet she'd balanced on her lap. Mitchell lifted a hand on her shoulder
and hung over his own lap. Everyone looked away.

Jorge crawled his hand to Josephina's breast in antic
fashion, fingers creeping and stumbling, and this time she
sat back in her chair, chewing her meat, not resisting him
or the joke.

Danielle asked, "Should we put on the news? If it's
really the Brooklyn Bridge, I mean, maybe there's something we should be doing, Mother?"

"Not today, darling. No. This is a party. How about
that music?" Hope said, but before Andrew effected it,
again the creak of a door—*all welcome!*

I bowed my own head and told myself I could simply
walk out, walk the streets and leave them to their party, go
to Montague Street and the old bookstore, to the magnolia
way past bloom on the corner of Clinton. Reenact different
days or see the bridge for myself. Keep to my course, my
counsel. I'd tell Hope I needed to walk off a headache, to
get some air. They'd talk of me, the strangeness of my
empty apartment, and Hope would struggle to quiet the
gossip. *A widow, yes. And she's so young.* But she couldn't explain how the lilac was too sweet and full in my throat and

nose, and how there was no room back here, a place so changed.

I looked up resigned to see the figure of Les, eclipsing us, taking what little air we had back here. Surely the wine had made me maudlin or it was Mitchell's face, on it the look of someone who could not win. But there was Mr. Coughlan: "I hope I am not interrupting you people. I got this very handsome invitation. I wanted—I mean I came to thank you for your kindness, but I am not one for parties, you see—"

Hope got to him first, enveloping him in her voice, her long bare arms, before he could finish making his excuses. She wouldn't miss the chance to steer the party somewhere new.

"Won't you at least let us feed you? I've worked so very hard on the food and Celia"—I stood from my chair and waved so he could see me—"has told us all so much about you. A man of the sea, if I recall right. A captain."

"Well, for a minute, for a minute then, for Miss Cassill's kindness. I did shave," he laughed. No one had anticipated the likes of him today, not even me: a man out of another time and glad to be. Yes, he wore his seaman's cap, the structure of which had held but whose fabric color was diluted, grayed, by sun and wind and sea and rain. His white cotton collared shirt and chinos were clean—crisp—but if you looked closely enough you'd find they were faintly spotted with the work he'd done, rust stains, oil, paint maybe; work he'd do now, if asked. He didn't need us or if so, for only so long. He was here on a lark or because he was hungry or curious. He was in no hurry. Hope loved him immediately, perceiving something in him more real and no-nonsense than she'd seen in a long time. She sat him at the head of the table and when he protested she said, "What if I share it with you?"

"It is Miss Cassill's table, isn't it?"

"I'll sit here, on the corner, next to Hope," I told him.

"And I'll sit next to you," said Leo, suddenly beside me, close to my ear.

Hope introduced everyone, and Mr. Coughlan nodded at every smile given him and said, "I am no good with names. Not because I'm old. I never have been."

"It's okay," said Darren. "We aren't very memorable."

"Is that so?" Mr. Coughlan asked and squinted at him, at everyone briefly, his hazel eyes more opaque in the sunlight than I'd remarked before, a blue cloud mixing through them as if to protect him from this day, maybe from the likes of us, preserving his sight for distances and views and places that lived inside him, that none of us would ever be in a position to know in the same way.

When he was offered wine, he asked for scotch. When I asked him how he liked it, he said, "Neat and hard and no trouble to you good people."

I told them all that Mr. Coughlan had been a merchant marine and ferryboat captain. I told them he'd been on a trip and had only just gotten back, and that he lived on the top floor. "You can see a bit of the harbor from there," I explained.

"Are you two related?" asked Darren.

"I have a daughter Miss Cassill's age," Mr. Coughlan answered. "She's not fond of her father. She'd like me to do as I'm told. I'm not so good at that either."

"Ah, a true man!" said Jorge, raising his glass and spilling his wine on his shirtfront. Two small birds, swallows maybe, dashed over our heads, complaining, a car horn sounded, and food was served to Mr. Coughlan, whiskey set next to his plate. "I feel like a king," he said to Hope, now seated beside him.

"A king returned from a crusade," I said.

"*Another* crusader?!" Blake interjected, lifting his glass.

"Well," he chewed slowly, "an inquiry maybe. . . . Thank you, Miss Cassill, for all you do, and you, ma'am. This is very good food."

"Hope can do anything," I said.

"What did you inquire about?" asked Jess.

"Work on ferryboats. Some beautiful boats operating right out there."

Evidently, Jess had been waiting for the right moment to say that he was a distant relative of Robert Fulton on his mother's side. It tumbled out of him.

"That so? He didn't invent the steamboat so much as make it better. He sank one of his first go's in a river, in France. It sank like a stone," Mr. Coughlan told us.

"He went there to be a painter. That's how he supported himself, doing portraits," said Jess.

"I think I heard that. My, this is the best food I've had in a long time."

Hope lit up: "No, no—"

"You couldn't support yourself as a fine art painter anywhere now. Could you?" Darren queried.

"Why not?" said Mr. Coughlan. "It depends on how grand you want to live."

"Did you find work?" Leo asked.

"Sort of." Mr. Coughlan explained that they'd hire him to babysit deckhands or assistant captains. They didn't know knots like he did. They weren't trained on the instruments much anymore, didn't have to be with the new technology, GPS. "They don't have the same respect," he said. "Not their fault. Computers make them lazy."

He chewed, swallowed. "One woman who has two touring boats—a sailer and a pleasure cruiser—said she might take me on if I subject myself to some tests." He sipped his whiskey. "But I'd be a fool not to fear those tests. And it's not a ferry, is it? I worked the Staten Island route many years ago. No one there remembers me. No one left to. But those ferries, those ferries are a marvel."

"Ugly," said Andrew.

"Maybe, but the Barberis, the two big ones?" He wiped his mouth with the back of his hand. "They have an egg-beater drive. Know what that is?" He looked at Jess.

"No, sir."

"A German design. Goddamn Germans." He grinned as he shook his head. "There's no rudder, no propeller in the normal sense. There are these big circular plates flush with the hull. From each plate comes down a number of paddles, six feet by two feet or so. They go into the water and by altering the pitch of the paddles and the speed they turn the plates, you go forward, back, slow, fast. Those big orange monsters can turn a 360 in their own length."

"Did you ever pilot one?" Leo asked.

"Not legally. They weren't in service when I was around. But on my recent trip I made some friends. They took pity on an old man. I held the wheel so to speak. Not for long."

"They could get in big trouble for that," said Jess.

"What are you?" Jorge asked of Danielle's young man, in the full swing of his drunkenness. "A woman?"

"Pay no attention to Jorge," said Josephina. "He is a big, stupid testicle."

Darren spit out his wine. *"Darling!"*

"Well," Mr. Coughlan said, "we won't tell on my friends at Whitehall. Will we? And who would believe me anyway?"

"I would. I do," said Hope, lightly bumping her shoulder to his. She loved the hardship his face showed it had survived, that he had the wrists and arms of a bigger man.

"And where did you captain?" asked Leo, plainly fascinated.

He recited places that most of us knew, but in this city backyard turned riotous garden with the afternoon light coming in sideways, it sounded the stuff of fantasy: Lake Champlain, Woods Hole, New London. New England by sea and lake. He told about the *Adirondack,* the oldest ferry in operation, how she'd been converted from steam to diesel. "She's still on the lake in Vermont. They know what they have in her. They take good care of her. My wife and I met on that boat, long before I became its captain."

"And where is your dear wife now?" asked Josephina.

"Buried with her family upstate."

"Ah, I'm sorry to hear."

"It's been a long time, but I dare say she loved the *Adirondack* as much as I did."

Hope's bandaged hand found my own under the table and gripped it as if to say, *like you,* maybe, yes, another widower, another loss observed, a course set. She didn't let go, and I felt the excitement and heat vibrate through her and through her son to the other side of me, whose hand had landed on my knee, when Mr. Coughlan had said Lake Champlain for the second time. I thought it an accident at first. I tensed but only for a moment, as Leo began to feel my knee's contours, bending time for me suddenly with the pressure of his fingertips, collapsing days. For me, and for Mr. Coughlan surely, even as we sat here so brightly well companioned, we were yet keeping our vigils. Death wasn't an abstraction. I'd done more than watch my husband vanish into it. I had gone there with him, as far as I could go, and in resurrecting him as I did, even now, I resurrected myself. A man more full of life than I was then or now, as alive as Leo's hand restless and oily from the food on my knee. Melville said that nothing exists by itself. "To enjoy bodily warmth, some part of you must be cold, for there is no quality in this world that is not what it is merely by contrast." Or by likeness—I would forever locate my husband in others, and in me, when anyone touched me with anything like love or loving desire. There was nothing to regret in it—or I could find nothing suddenly, nothing at all. Mr. Coughlan might have compared Hope's food to his wife's, whose cooking never came up wanting. We held on to our ghosts as we held hard to each other. My husband had not lived as long as our love had, not long enough to disappoint me in real ways. I knew that by now. We weren't tested by boredom or the demands of raising children, but even if we had been, for however many years, it may have only increased the fact, or what was to me a fact, that it's never easy to separate the living and the dead—we living are in some part best expressed by our dead.

Hope now took my hand into both of hers, as if she would drag the chill out of me, as the day faded and Mr. Coughlan talked on and Angie's head fell on her husband's shoulder and his head onto hers.

Mr. Coughlan went on describing why he'd chosen ferries and would again. "Some will tell me it's all done. I blackened the eye of one guy who said that to me only a few weeks ago. They forget I'm from a generation that wasn't afraid to hit and get hit back and no one called the damned police or involved lawyers. I told him to tell me that again. You, Miss Cassill, you understand, I think?" He'd spoken to his daughter since he'd returned then, and he winked at me as proof. I blushed and Leo's hand moved up my thigh. "You see, people change when they get on the boat. It's like an old friend. Simple back and forth. Commuters— you pick out the same faces. Hello, goodbye, hello again, goodbye again. Weather changes, but that doesn't. No one squalling at you over the loudspeaker. Birds scream. Kids scream back. Until recently out here you could stay on the boat both ways, stay on as long you'd like, keep crossing, seeing what there was to see, you could put your car right on there with you—" He leaned into the table at which we all sat, enjoying that we'd become subdued with the food and the wine and him. He didn't have to hide where he most wanted to be, but here he was, for now, surrounded and talking with reverence not all of us knew or had occasion to know of the simple back and forth, of attachments that sustain us without apology, that drive us, no matter the years, all while asking us to cross with him—why not?— imagine it, the tides of coming and going, the distances and views and places, and the love, such love—before saying goodbye to us, goodbye for now.

ACKNOWLEDGMENTS

Great thanks to Picador, the best house on the block, and to all the imaginative, never-say-die people who make it go: Stephen Morrison, James Meader, Anna deVries, and Devon Mazzone.

To my own Melville: Thank you for taking on the challenge of living with this writer and editor (which means living with many writers). You always have my back. You are my balance, the song in the house.

Thanks to Jess Walter, Ron Hansen, and Will Blythe, who loved this book and its heroine, Celia, when my own sometimes unpredictable nature (and hers) got in the way. Don't know better writers or better friends.

To Warren Frazier, the most sublime, capable, and forgiving literary agent and ally a woman writer could have. To my family, my parents, who are my heart. Pop, a man from Vermont, can do anything better than just about anyone, from percentages to parallel parking—blindfolded. He has always been my first reader, my best critic, the rousing march in my ears. He is well met in my beautiful, ingenious, and wildly generous mother, who fights the gray off every day. These two have always bent the world into wondrous shapes for all of us who know them and have given me colors and sustenance and room (after room) in which to write, hope, persist. And to my sisters, Meredith and Ellen, warriors of love and light both, and my sweet brother-in-law Tom—they never fail to cheer me on even when I resist cheer.

And my thanks to my other family, the one I've found along the way: David Slocum, my brilliant best friend, who has to hear it all, even when he'd rather not. To glorious Rebecca Rotert-Shaw, so full of music and poetry and my kind of life and love, resilience and resignation. To Eli Dickson, my safe place in any storm and the sky after it goes. To Lee Froehlich, who bamboozles me every time with that line about the life of the mind, who reminds me of the joys of eccentricity. To Chris Napolitano, the best magazine editor in town, an adventurer who changes the frequency in any room, leaves us all buzzing. And to Anthony Vargas, my assistant, my teammate, and one of the finest readers of fiction or nonfiction around; to Tom

Woodring, whose smarts and practical wisdom steady and inspire me; to Kate Strasburg, who can't help but be an angel; to Gayle Pemberton, my talented teacher, fellow romantic, and co-conspirator in the resistance; and to Caroline McDaniel, who never fails to show up, who's a real reader, a real woman, a sorceress in fact.

Finally, there are the writers I've worked with over the years who've become friends, family too: Margaret Atwood, James Ellroy, Jonathan Ames, Carmela Ciuraru, Jonathan Lethem, Joyce Carol Oates, Richard Ford, Jane Smiley, Simon Winchester, and Rick Russo. Ten stories of gratitude for your example, for the heights you can't help reaching for every day, for your faith in me as an editor, friend, and more.

blog and newsletter

For literary discussion, author insight,
book news, exclusive content,
recipes and giveaways, visit the
Weidenfeld & Nicolson blog and
sign up for the newsletter at:

www.wnblog.co.uk

For breaking news, reviews and exclusive competitions
Follow us @wnbooks
Find us facebook.com/WNfiction

BRANCH	DATE
L/	1/14